# Workshop on Natural Language Processing 2014

**Held as part of the 5th Information Systems Research Working Days (JISIC 2014)**



## Quito, Ecuador
## 20 – 24 October 2014

**Editors:**

**M. Hernandez**
**J. Aguiar Pontes**

ISBN: 978-1-63439-925-8

**Printed from e-media with permission by:**

Curran Associates, Inc.
57 Morehouse Lane
Red Hook, NY 12571

CURRAN ASSOCIATES INC. proceedings.com

**Some format issues inherent in the e-media version may also appear in this print version.**



Printed by Curran Associates, Inc. (2015)



Association for Computational Linguistics
209 N. Eighth Street
Stroudsburg, Pennsylvania 18360

Phone: 1-570-476-8006
Fax: 1-570-476-0860

acl@aclweb.org

**Additional copies of this publication are available from:**

Curran Associates, Inc.
57 Morehouse Lane
Red Hook, NY 12571 USA
Phone: 845-758-0400
Fax: 845-758-2634
Email: curran@proceedings.com
Web: www.proceedings.com

# W001-2014

# Proceedings of the Workshop on Natural Language Processing in the 5th Information Systems Research Working Days (JISIC 2014)

October 20th to 24th, 2014
Faculty of Systems Engineering. National Polytechnic School of Ecuador.
Quito, Ecuador

# Preface

The Workshop on Natural Language Processing (NLP) is an annual meeting organized in the Information Systems Research Working Days by Faculty of Systems Engineering of the National Polytechnic School of Ecuador. JISIC 2014 is the fifth meeting in the series and was held in Quito, Ecuador, from October 20-24, 2014.

This Workshop aims to spread in Latin America the knowledge of the latest techniques involved on data preparation and algorithms for building applications on Natural Language Processing. The North American Chapter of the Association for Computational Linguistics (NAACL) has endorsed the event.

The lecturers have been invited to write papers on all aspects of computational approaches to Natural Language Processing. The papers received have been revised and prepared to compose this issue.

We thank all lecturers and participants who have contributed and made this publication possible. We also appreciate and give a special thanks to the support from the Association for Computational Linguistics (ACL).

We hope you enjoy reading the memories of the Workshop!

M.Sc. Myriam Hernandez
Computer researcher of Natural Language Processing
Dean of the Faculty of Systems Engineering of the National Polytechnic School of Ecuador

Dr. Josafá Aguiar Pontes
Computer scientist of Natural Language Processing
Prometeo researcher at the National Polytechnic School of Ecuador

## Conference Co-Chairs

MSc. Myriam Hernández
Dr. Josafá Pontes

## Conference Revisors

Dr. José Gómez S.
Dr. Rafael Muñoz
Dr. Patricio Martínez B.
Dra. Paloma Moreda P.
Ing. Fernando Peregrino

## Invited Speakers

Dr. Sunil Kopparapu (TCS Innovations Labs - Mumbai)
Dr. Mauricio Espinoza (Universidad de Cuenca)

# Tabla de contenido


Preface .......... 3

Conference Co-Chairs .......... 4

Conference Revisors .......... 4

Invited Speakers .......... 4

Conference Program Workshop NLP .......... 6

Corpus annotation methodology for citation classification in scientific literature .......... 7

Bilingual Sentence Alignment of a Parallel Corpus by Using English as a Pivot Language .......... 13

Language Technologies for Suicide Prevention in Social Media .......... 21

A Supervised Approach for Sentiment Analysis using Skipgrams .......... 30

Emotion Detection from text: A Survey .......... 37

## Conference Program

## Workshop NLP

*Towards the production of a corpus for content analysis of references in scientific literature*
Ing. MSc. M. Hernández. Escuela Politécnica Nacional. Ecuador.

*Bilingual sentence alignment of a parallel corpus by using English as a pivot language*
Dr. Josafá Pontes. Escuela Politécnica Nacional. Ecuador.

*Language Technologies for Suicide Prevention in Social Media*
Dr. José Gómez. University of Alicante. Spain.

*Sentiment analysis in the Web 2.0 using skipgrams.*
Ing. Javi Fernández. University of Alicante. Spain.

*Emotion Detection from text: A Survey*
Ing. Lea Canales. University of Alicante. Spain.

**Invited speaker:**
*Advances in speech and natural language*
Dr. Sunil Kopparapu

# Corpus annotation methodology for citation classification in scientific literature

Myriam Hernández Álvarez
Escuela Politécnica Nacional
Facultad de Ingeniería de Sistemas
Quito, Ecuador
myriam.hernandez@epn.edu.ec

José Gómez Soriano
Universidad de Alicante
Dpto. de Lenguajes y Sistemas Informáticos
Alicante, España
jmgomez@ua.es

## Abstract

Since, at the moment there is not a gold-standard annotated corpus for this objective, it is necessary to build one, to allow generation and testing of automatic systems for classifying the purpose or function of a citation referenced in an article. The development of this kind of corpus is subject to two conditions: the first one is to present a clear and unambiguous classification scheme. The second one is to secure an initial manual process of labeling to reach a sufficient inter-coder agreement among annotators to validate the annotation scheme and to be able to reproduce it even with coders who do not know in depth the topic of the analyzed articles. This paper proposes and validates a methodology for corpus annotation for citation classification in scientific literature that facilitate annotation and produces substantial inter-annotator agreement.

## 1 Introduction

Not all citations have the same effect in a citing article. The impact of a cited paper may vary considerably. It could go from being a criticism, or a starting point for a job or simply an acknowledge of the work of other authors. However, accepted methods available today are variations of citation counting where all citations are considered equal and are evaluated with the same weight. Current methods of measuring impact fall into one of three techniques: simple count of citations (more citations, more impact); co citation which adds as a measure of similarity between two works the number of common documents that cited them; and the Google's PageRank that measure citation relevance using the relevance and frequency of the citing document. Not all citations are equal, so they should not weigh equally in the impact calculation. None of the above mentioned counting methods takes into account whether the citation context is positive or negative, the purpose of the citing article, or if the citation has or not have influence on it.

It becomes important to identify more complete metrics that take into account the content about cited work to assess its impact and relevance. It is necessary the construction of a new impact index enriched with qualitative criteria regarding the citation. This process requires a content analysis of the context containing citations to obtain certain important features such as intent or purpose of the citing author when made the reference.

Content analysis is a group of procedures to recollect and organized information in standard format to make inferences about its characteristics and meaning using manual or automatic methods (Ding, Zhang, Chambers, Song, Wang, and Zhai, 2014). This analysis could be automatic starting from a tagged corpus to build a model.

Since, there is not a gold-standard annotated corpus for citation analysis data, it is necessary to work in the generation of one in order to facilitate collaborative work and results comparison among researches. Development of a corpus starts from the definition of a citation classification scheme that considers function (purpose), polarity (disposition) and influence of cited paper to produce a reliable and reproducible data set that could be the basis for future work in this area. This tagged corpus will allow overcoming problems currently present that make very difficult to strengthen collaborative efforts in this field (Hernández y Gómez, 2014). Present problems are, for instance, the lack of a standard classification scheme and of sufficient public data available such that researchers could test their systems and compare results.

According to Arstein and Poesio (2008), a corpus is reliable if annotators agree in the assigned categories because it displays a similar understanding of the classification scheme. This criterion is a prerequisite to demonstrate validity of a scheme. If there is no consistency among the obtained results, the representation may be inappropriate for the data.

In our experiment, we pose a scheme to classify citation functions and we defined an annotation methodology to allow a greater accuracy in the process to facilitate decision-making and generate a greater inter-coder agreement. The subject of this article focus in the proposed annotation methodology which could be applied to any scheme with the only condition that the scheme is not ambiguous i.e. its categories are clearly differentiated.

## 2 Method

We applied different citation classification schemes according to citation function. The condition for these schemes were that categories were well distinguished.

In this process, we detected two sources or error that affected results and did not allow good agreement among coders. One had to do with usage by the annotators of context of different length, which lend them to obtain discrepant results; the other was lack of clarity in the analyzed articles that made difficult to find enough sense in text to reach a unique citation classification.

We corrected the first factor setting fixed criteria for determining context length. Hernández and Gómez, (2014) highlighted the need for defining context in view of argument detection, so the context include all sentences around citation that are talking about it. However, due to the complexity of this task, we decided to replace argument detection by fixing a context delimited by a complete paragraph. The rationale for this decision was that, by definition, a paragraph is a group of related sentences about the same idea. We assumed that author's purpose when making a citation could be found using cue words and ontological concepts that are within the same paragraph.

To avoid the second error source, we proposed a new annotation methodology to help coders to organize the ideas expressed in the text, to take them to decide citation function classification in an orderly way. With the proposed annotation methodology, we could achieve a minimized human effort with a clear understanding of the structure of the presented ideas, so that we could generate a natural association of functions and their classes. As an additional advantage, the methodology includes detection of patterns formed by lexical values (cue words) and ontological classes related to a function. We could convert this information to regular expressions to be the foundation for automatic citation classification. Without regular expressions, to annotate a corpus of sufficient size we would require too much effort to detect patterns statistically. In fact, in the initial experiments, the original intention for pattern use was to annotate them in conjunction with function definition, so that, these patterns included in the corpus, would facilitate model detection in an automatic tagging process. We changed this approach and decided to pre-annotate first in an attempt to improve a very low annotation agreement, and with this change, we obtained a new and more effective way to data-set annotation.

The proposed annotation methodology consists of two phases. In the first, we perform a pre-annotation process in which we define patterns. These patterns help coders to understand structure of sentences within context and help them to define citation function. In this step, the annotator detects a sentence type, saving the original sentence order to maintain relevant information related with citation purpose. Zock, 2012, presented patterns that link ontological and syntactic categories to generate sentences maintaining the author's original intention. These techniques allow associating between purpose and an ontological pattern. We adapt this basic idea to the solution or our problem and develop concepts and notation to our method.

In the pre-annotation stage, coders identify manually ontological and lexical patterns that are near of citations within the content defined as a paragraph. A pattern consists of a fixed part and a variable part. The fixed part is underlined and corresponds to cue words related to a function. We label the variable part as XML, according to ontological concepts as cited work, author, theory, action, method, used material, concept, task, result, quoted text, assumption, person, experiment, positive feature, negative feature, etc. We design the group of tags so that we cover without ambiguity the largest number of possibilities.

For instance, if we have the text: "This feature set is based on Dong and Schäfer, 2011." Pre-annotation result will be: "<material>this feature set</material> is based on <cited>Dong and Schäfer, 2011</cited>." In addition, the pattern will be "MATERIAL is based CITED", where MATERIAL and CITED are the variable part and "is based" is the fixed part that corresponds to cue words. In this case, it is clear that citation function has to do with the use other author's material as a base for own work.

Other sentences can be generated with this pattern, for instance, "The algorithm is based in the Vector Space Model – VSM (Salton et al., 1975)". This sentence pre-annotated is "<material>The algorithm</material> is based in the Vector Space Model – VSM <cited> (Salton et al., 1975)</cited>". The pattern is the same that the one in the previous example "MATERIAL is based CITED", with the equal function type than last example because pattern is identical.

Fixed part is a skip-gram with 1 to 4 length. Each group of words is a sequence. A skip-gram, according to Guthrie, Allison, Liu, Guthrie, and Wilks (2006), is a generalization of an n-gram, where text leave not considered spaces, while a skip-gram does consider spaces between word sequences.

## 2.1 Examples of pre-annotation process

To understand better the pre-annotation scheme, we show three examples of how to apply it to the context of scientific citations. First, consider the following sentence containing a citation:

"We compare our zone classifier to a reimplementation of Teufel and Moens's NB classifier and features on their original Computational Linguistic corpus".

After applying the ontological pattern annotation scheme, we obtained the following result:

"<author>We<\author> compare our <material>zone classifier<\material> to a reimplementation of <cited>Teufel and Moens<\cited>'s <material>NB classifier<\material> and <material>features<material> on their original <material>Computational Linguistic corpus<\material>".

Its ontological pattern is:" AUTHOR compare our MATERIAL to CITED MATERIAL"

This pattern contains a skip-gram, which is formed by two word sequences: "compare our" and "to". The idea behind the whole sentence is that the authors compare their own material with a cited material. The classification of author's sentiment is not part of this work, but the pattern clearly reveals a comparison between authors' contribution with other researchers'.

Let us take a second example out of the literature to illustrate our method. Consider the following paragraph containing a citation:

"Comprehension-based summarization, e.g. Kintsch and Van Dijk (1978) and Brown et al. (1983), is the most ambitious model of automatic summarization, requiring a complete understanding of the text. Due to the failure of rule-based NLP and knowledge representation, other less knowledge-intensive methods now dominate".

Annotating this paragraph, we have:

"Comprehension-based summarization, e.g. <cited1>Kintsch and Van Dijk (1978)</cited1> and <cited2>Brown et al. (1983)<\cited2>, is the most ambitious model of automatic summarization, requiring a complete understanding of the text. Due to the failure of <method>rule-based NLP<\method> and <method>knowledge representation<\method>, other less knowledge-intensive methods now dominate".

Its ontological pattern is:

"CITED ambitious * .Due to * failure of METHOD

CITED ambitious * .Due to * failure of METHOD".

The pattern contains a skip-gram having three word sequences: "ambitious", ".Due to" and "failure of". The skip-grams are indicated by a star symbol * in between the sequences. The variable parts are two: <cited> and <method>. The idea behind this pattern is that the cited researchers were ambitious, but they failed on the authors' point of view. This pattern clearly reveals authors' negative impression or a weakness regarding the cited work.

Finally, we present a third example by taking the following sentence containing a citation:

"The baseline score shown in bold, is obtained with no context window and is comparable to the results reported by Athar (2011)".

Applying our annotation scheme, we produce:

"The <result>baseline score<\result>, shown in bold, is obtained with no context window and is comparable to the <result>results<\result> reported by <cited>Athar (2011)<\cited>".

Its ontological pattern is:

"RESULT is * comparable to RESULT CITED".

Again, the pattern contains a skip-gram having two word sequences: "is" and "comparable to". Additionally, it contains three variable parts: <result> <result> <cited>. From this pattern, we clear see that authors are comparing their results with other researchers'. Independently of the function classification, the ontological patterns are supposed to reveal the authors' intention concerning the cited work.

The application of this strategy allows identifying punctual lexical entries and their relation to semantic features. An ontological pattern here is a structure that conveys authors' purpose to cite. By using that, we expect not only to obtain a good level of agreement among the annotators, but also to minimize the human effort needed for annotating papers and populate a big corpus by converting the patterns into regular expressions.

## 3 Experiment setup and results

Three annotators collaborated. The annotation process comply three requirements in order to achieve reliability and reproducibility (Krippendorff, 2004). The annotators had a profile that allow them a good understanding of the scientific texts in computational linguistics; they worked in an independent way and they had a clear function classification scheme with detail instructions.

To test annotation reliability, we measured inter-annotator agreement in a small section of the corpus; the same people must review this sample. It is necessary to achieve a good rate in this agreement because it certifies that the process is reliable and reproducible and that results may be generalized to the complete process in which probably are going to work new annotators and not only the ones that coded the trial (Artstein y Poesio, 2008).

We analyzed 101 citations to classify them according to their function without pre-annotation and 101 different citations with pre-annotation. We measured inter-annotator agreement in each case.

## 4 Results and discussion

We computed Fleiss, Krippendorff indexes and Pairwise average using Geertzen, J. (2012) software. Calculations were made for processes without and with pre-annotation. Pre-annotation applies the explained methodology. We present results in Table 1 and 2.

### 4.1 Results without applying pre-annotation

The experiment had 3 annotators, 101 cases, and 1 variable with 303 decisions.

| Fleiss | Krippendorff | Pairwise avg. |
|---|---|---|
| A_obs = 0.554<br>A_exp= 0.274<br>Kappa = 0.386 | D_obs = 0.446<br>D_exp = 0.728<br>Alpha = 0.388 | % agr = 55.4<br>Kappa=0.405 |

Table 1: Results for inter-annotator agreement without pre-annotation

### 4.2 Results applying pre-annotation

The experiment had 3 annotators, 101 cases, and 1 variable with 303 decisions.

| Fleiss | Krippendorff | Pairwise avg. |
|---|---|---|
| A_obs=0.845<br>A_esp=0.365<br>Kappa=0.756 | D_obs = 0.155<br>D_esp = 0.637<br>Alpha = 0.756 | % agr= 84.5<br>Kappa=0.756 |

Table 2: Results for inter-annotator agreement with pre-annotation

## 5 Conclusions and future work

Results without pre-annotation presented low inter-annotator agreement values. We could explicate this, due to the complexity that have the process for defining functions in a medium granularity scheme with at least five functions. We consider that a five-function scheme allows differentiating citation functions. We tested the methodology with a scheme with this number of classes. Annotators read carefully the articles but, without a pre-annotation process, results were poor because annotators had to take into account too many details and even with a through reading, text structure is difficult to appreciate.

There is a big improvement in inter-annotator agreement using the proposed methodology that includes a pre-annotation process of a citation context with a fixed one-paragraph length. The previous process of extracting ontological concepts and cue words allowed that annotator could see more clearly sentence structure and facilitate decision making about the citation function classification. The result is a very significant enhancement of inter-annotator agreement that validates the use of the proposed methodology.

With the proposed annotation methodology the agreement percentage, without a random correction is 84.5% and Kappa index is 0,756. According Landis and Koch (1977), a K = 0,756 corresponds to a substantial annotator agreement, while the initial results, without pre-annotation corresponded to a minimum value which was not enough to keep on working in the topic.

We plan to annotate a sufficient number of articles using this methodology together with a non-ambiguous and complete scheme of annotation. The annotations generated, ontological patterns and cue words will serve to mine in an automatic way in a non-annotated corpus. Thus, we will continue to expand a basic corpus for the development of research in citation function analysis.

Our intention is to make available to the scientific community this dataset to facilitate research in order to develop better systems to evaluate the citation impact in scientific literature. The purpose of these systems will be to take into account new factors that can be incorporated in the calculation of indexes to better assess function, significance and disposition of an author towards the scientific work of another that was referenced.

## Acknowledgement

This research work has been partially funded by the Spanish Government and the European Commission through the project, ATTOS (TIN2012-38536-C03- 03), LEGOLANG (TIN2012-31224), SAM (FP7- 611312) and FIRST (FP7-287607).

## References

Artstein, R., and Poesio, M. "Inter-coder agreement for computational linguistics." Computational Linguistics 34.4 (2008): 555-596.

Ding, Y., Zhang, G., Chambers, T., Song, M., Wang, X., & Zhai, C. (2014). Content-based citation analysis: The next generation of citation analysis. Journal of the Association for Information Science and Technology.

Geertzen, J. (2012). Inter-Rater Agreement with multiple raters and variables. Retrieved November 16, 2014, from https://mlnl.net/jg/software/ira

Guthrie, D., Allison, B., Liu, W., Guthrie, L., & Wilks, Y. (2006). A closer look at skip-gram modelling. In Proceedings of the 5th international Conference on Language Resources and Evaluation (LREC-2006) (pp. 1-4).

Hernández, M., & Gómez, J. M. (2014). Survey in sentiment, polarity and function analysis of citation. ACL 2014, 102.

Krippendorff, K. 2004. Reliability in content analysis: Some common misconceptions and recommendations. Human Communication Research, 30(3):411–433.

Landis, J. R., & Koch, G. G. (1977). The measurement of observer agreement for categorical data. Biometrics, 159-174.

Zock, M., & Tesfaye, D. (2012, December). Automatic index creation to support navigation in lexical graphs encoding part_of relations. In 24th International Conference on Computational Linguistics (p. 33).

# Bilingual Sentence Alignment of a Parallel Corpus by Using English as a Pivot Language

Josafá de Jesus Aguiar Pontes
National Polytechnic School of Ecuador, Quito, Ecuador
Ladrón de Guevara E11-253, Quito 170517
josafa@furui.cs.titech.ac.jp

Abstract

Statistically training a machine translation model requires a parallel corpus containing a huge amount of aligned sentence pairs in both languages. However, it is not easy to obtain such a corpus when English is not the source or the target language. The European Parliament parallel corpus contains only English sentence alignments with 20 European languages, missing alignments for other 190 language pairs. A previous method using sentence length information is not enough reliable to produce alignments for training statistical machine translation models. Hybrid methods combining sentence length and bilingual dictionary information may produce better results, but dictionaries may not be affordable. Thus, we introduce a technique which aligns non-English corpora from the European Parliament by using English as a pivot language without a bilingual dictionary. Our technique has been illustrated with French and Spanish, resulting on an equivalent performance with the existing one in the original English-French and English-Spanish corpora.

## 1 Introduction

Obtaining a parallel corpus of aligned sentence pairs is an important task to further work for human translators and several natural language processing applications such as statistical machine translation (Brown et al, 1990; Melamed, 1998), cross-lingual information retrieval (Davis and Dunning, 2995; Landauer and Littman, 1990; Oard, 1997) and lexical acquisition (Gale and Church, 1991; Melamed, 1997), to mention some. Bilingual corpora are useful for human translators to search for a chunk of text in a source language and to find its corresponding translation into a target language. From the machine's standpoint, one of the most common applications is on training statistical models for machine translation. In the translation domain, no matter human or machine, they both need a very huge amount of aligned sentence pairs in order to find appropriate word combination that enable them to produce good translations.

Each language is a world of symbols made of its own set of words and their possible combinations that lead to a meaning from the native speakers' point of view. A parallel corpus comes as a map in between two languages, indicating which set of word combinations in a source language produces another set of words in a target language. Being so, we assume that the more sentence pairs there are in a corpus, the better is the mapping between the two languages and consequently, the better are the derived translations from it. Therefore, a huge amount of translated sentence pairs is essential.

Due to this growing demand, a number of parallel corpora have become available within the last decade, for instance the Europarl corpus

(Koehn, 2005[1]), the News from OPUS[2], the JRC-Acquis corpus3, the MultiUN corpus4 and the EU Official Journal EU Official Journal Multilingual Legal Text in 22 European Languages (Gale and Church, 1993), which are freely downloadable for research purposes. The Europarl corpus in particular is a parallel corpus extracted from the proceedings of the European Parliament. It consists of texts in 21 European languages, where English is the only language with which the other languages are aligned. Some of the remaining resources above mentioned do contain alignments between all combinations of language pairs; however, the quality of these alignments is questionable given that the alignment method utilized for most of them is solely based on sentence length information (Varga et al., 2005). Our experiments show that such alignments may present around 90% of precision. Obviously, the performance depends on the internal arrangement of the sentences being provided as input. Although the information of a good bilingual dictionary may be used to enhance the performance of an aligner (Schmid, 1994[5]), it is not normally available for free, even less when none of the two languages involved is English. In other words, most of the freely available non-English parallel corpora have not been aligned with the use of the respective bilingual dictionaries and therefore the quality relies basically on sentence length information.

Although the Europarl corpus has also been aligned with sentence length feature, there are underlying alignment information and noise removal which make the final quality to be very high. First, its alignment is simplified by the fact that the texts are originally available in a paragraph aligned format. Second, each paragraph is typically small, containing from 2 to 5 sentences only. Third, much noise is removed by discarding an utterance of a speaker when the number of paragraphs in it differs in the two languages being aligned. The prior data preparation done by the underlying paragraph information combined with the noise removal technique leads to an alignment of excellent quality. According to our experiments its precision reaches more than 99%.

Each corpus contains approximately 2 million English sentences and it is pairwise aligned with 20 other European languages. Since each parallel corpus is independently aligned, the number of sentences in each bitext is not the same across the language pairs. Most of the difference is due to the utterance removal process described above which occurred prior to the alignment. Consequently, not all the English sentences of a corpus (e.g. the English part from the English-French bitext) are present in the other corpus (e.g. the English part from the English-Spanish bitext). In other words, considering the English-French and the English-Spanish corpora for example, not all of the English sentences from the former can be found in the latter and viceversa. It means there are sentence insertions, deletions and substitutions when we consider two English corpora coming from diferent aligned language pairs of the same Europarl corpus.

It is unreasonable to expect the same alignment precision of two non-English texts from the Europarl corpus just by using the sentence length information. The prior sentence insertions, deletions and substitutions introduce an observable noise when comparing a pair of non-English texts, making harder the work of the aligner. In fact, our experiments point out to a precision of only 90% given an amount of such a data. As previously stated, a bilingual dictionary

---

[1] Europarl, 2005. www.statmt.org/europarl/

[2] Tiedemann, 2009 http://opus.lingfil.uu.se/ECB.php

[3] Ralf et al., 2006. http://ipsc.jrc.ec.europa.eu/index.php?id=198

[4] Eisele and Chen, 2010 www.dfki.de/lt/publication_show.php?id=4790

[5] www.cis.unimuenchen.de/~schmid/tools/TreeTagger/

may be helpful to improve this figure, but unfortunately, good ones are very expensive[6] to be affordable by developing countries for research purposes.

Taking these constraints into consideration, we have developed a sentence alignment method which exempts the use a bilingual dictionary when a multilingual corpus has previously and efficiently been aligned with English. This is the case of the Europarl corpus which contains only English sentence alignments with other languages. This paper is organized in the following way: In the Section 2 we describe our method. Section 3 contains the experiments for validating the method. Section 4 brings the results and the related discussions. In Section 5 we point out to conclusions and future work.

## 2 Bilingual Sentence Alignment Algorithm

This section is divided into two parts. First, we define the core algorithm and explain which type of corpus is needed in order to utilize the method. Then we provide additional details of the algorithm for implementation.

### 2.1 Assumptions and the Core of the Algorithm

We assume that we use a multilingual corpus which has previously been aligned with at least one language. Let's say that English is the pivot language. We want to obtain sentence alignments between any two foreign (non-English) languages of this data. Let's illustrate our method with French and Spanish. By assumption, there are available an English-French and an English-Spanish corpora, where each corpus is individually sentence aligned with English as the pivot language. Although the majority of the English sentences of both corpora are the same, not all of them need to be so. In other words, we allow for insertions, deletions and substitutions of English sentences on both sides and therefore the number of sentences in both bitexts are different. This is the case of the Europarl corpus.

Our method is very simple. It basically consists of creating a new alignment between two English corpora while keeping the reference to the original alignment information in order to map from one foreign language to the other. For instance, suppose that we need to obtain a French-Spanish sentence alignment. Since English is the common language for both English-French and English-Spanish corpora, the English texts are first aligned with each other. The original English-French and the English-Spanish alignment information is the basis for the new English-English sentence alignment to work properly.

Four cases are possible during this alignment process. First, the simplest cases consist of those sentences which are exactly the same in both corpora (one-to-one cases). Second, the first side of the corpus contains a short sentence which needs to be concatenated with one or more adjacent sentences in order to produce the same sequence of characters as the second side (many-to-one cases). Third, the first side of the corpus contains a long sentence while the second contains a short sentence which needs to be concatenated with one or more adjacent sentences in order to result in the same sequence of characters as the first side (one-to-many cases). And finally, there are cases where a sentence of a side is not a substring of the sentence from the other side or vice-versa and therefore these sentence pairs are not easily aligned (one-to-zero or zero-to-one cases).

In spite of this, we still try to find an alignment for them, given that we allow for insertions, deletions and substitutions of English sentences in the input data at both sides. In such a case, our algorithm temporarily stores the sentence positions of both unaligned sentences in order to perform the following procedures. A pointer to the sentence of the first side refers to a string that is compared with each one of the next 500 sentences of the second side. If found somewhere, an alignment is obtained and the algorithm proceeds from the next sentence position on, at both sides. Otherwise, a pointer to the sentence of the second side is used for comparison with each of the next

[6] ELRA: SCI-FRES-EURADIC
http://catalog.elra.info/product_info.php?cPath=42_45&products_id=668

500 sentences of the first side. If found somewhere, an alignment is obtained and the algorithm proceeds from the next sentence position on, at both sides. However, when no alignment can be obtained after trying these thousand times, we assume there is no way of aligning those pointed sentences with any other adjacent sentence of the opposite side. Then it continues the execution of the aligner from the next sentence positions on, right after the pointers.

Note that we assume the number 500 as a generous search limit between the two texts, given that during the preparation of the Europarl corpus, each paragraph typically contained only a few sentences and the discarded utterances occurred only when the number of paragraphs in them differed in the original two languages being aligned.

During the execution of this algorithm, the history of all sentence positions having successful English-English alignments is stored. We call it ladder alignment history, making reference to the Hunalign tool developed by Varga et al. It contains a list of pair of numbers, representing the sentence position of both English corpora having successful alignment with each other. This is the main information needed for aligning the pairs of French and Spanish sentences of our example. Note that the sentence positions on the left stand for the English corpus originally aligned with French, while the sentence positions on the right stand for the English corpus originally aligned with Spanish. Therefore, each pair of numbers represents the alignment between French and Spanish sentences. While the number of lines in the ladder alignment history represent the number of newly aligned sentences.

Also note that the sentence positions of the new alignment are relative to the original alignments in the English-French and English-Spanish parallel corpora. It means that the original alignment errors are also preserved. A new alignment error is produced whenever an x English sentence is correctly aligned with French but incorrectly aligned with Spanish or vice-versa. This is a one-to-one error type, and it is due to a single bad pre-existing alignment which is found either in the English-French or in the English-Spanish corpus. Now, let's consider the case where a y English sentence is originally misaligned with both French and Spanish at the same time. The newly produced alignment accounts for both as a single error, given that the French sentence is misaligned with a single Spanish sentence. This is a two-to-one error type.

$$\#\text{New alignment errors} \leq \sum(\#\text{alignment errors of Pivot-Foreign1}) + \sum(\#\text{alignment errors of Pivot-Foreign2}) \quad \text{(Equation 1)}$$

It implies that the number of alignment errors produced by our algorithm is usually less than the sum of all misalignments for each original bitext. In the worst case, there is no two-to-one error type, i.e. the sentences of both parallel corpora do not contain any overlapping misalignments. In such a case, the number of new alignment errors is the sum of all misalignments present in both original corpora. This idea is expressed by Equation (1), where Pivot indicates the common language of the original alignments (i.e. English), while Foreign1 and Foreign2 represent the pair of foreign languages that our algorithm aligns, being illustrated here by the French and Spanish languages.

### 2.2 Additional Details of the Algorithm

Now that we have presented the core of our algorithm, we introduce some further details which allow our algorithm to work efficiently. When an English-English alignment is one-to-many or many-to-one, a special symbol is added in between two adjacent sentences. The amount of special symbols indicates how many short adjacent sentences are concatenated together in order to correspond to the same string of characters as the long sentence. We also store the information whether the concatenated short sentences are on the left (English-French corpus) or on the right (English-Spanish corpus), so that our algorithm can later reproduce the same number of sentence concatenations to the adjacent sentences of a corpus. This information is stored in the ladder alignment history as a pair of numbers, where the first one stands for the number of concatenated English sentences originating from the English-French corpus while the second is the number of concatenated English sentences originating from the English-Spanish corpus.

However, the ladder alignment history at this point is not yet ready. Some wrong alignment might have been introduced during the English-English sentence alignment process, which is normal for any aligner. We do here a post-processing which confirms whether every pair of aligned English sentences contains exactly the same string of characters. The wrongly aligned sentences are removed. This is the way we use for automatically validating the produced alignments. We do so by fetching the respective pair of English sentences whose indexes are present in the ladder alignment history. They are extracted from both English texts, respectively from the English-French and the English-Spanish corpora. Then, we remove the special symbols used for sentence concatenation of one-to-many or many-to-one cases in order to perform the string comparisons. Finally, we preserve only those lines containing exactly the same English sentences, and consequently producing a clean ladder alignment history.

We use the sentence alignment information present in it to obtain the aligned foreign sentence pairs. It tells the sentence index of the first foreign language which matches with the sentence index of the second one. It also tells on a sentence basis how many adjacent sentences of a corpus need to be concatenated in order to fully correspond to its translation. The work of the algorithm from this point on is basically to read the pieces of data from the following three files: ladder alignment history, first and second foreign language corpora. It combines the sentences together in order to produce the aligned parallel corpus. It finalizes the process by removing null sentence pairs and those having null translations.

## 3 Experiments

We want to quantify the efficiency of our algorithm to produce an aligned parallel corpus of non-English language pairs given that the sentences in both languages have been previously aligned with English. We illustrate the performance of our method by using the French and the Spanish texts from the Europarl corpus, which had been previously aligned with English on an individual basis. The English-French and the English-Spanish parallel corpora are freely available for download.

We have created a reference French-Spanish parallel corpus from the Europarl data. We extracted the first 14,941 sentences from the French corpus and the first 14,356 sentences from the Spanish corpus, totalizing 29,297 monolingual sentences. This alignment has been done in three steps. First, each corpus has been individually lemmatized by using the TreeTagger software. Second, we utilized a sentence aligner software called Hunalign to produce the sentence alignments, providing both lemmatized corpora as input and a French-Spanish bilingual dictionary of 69,231 entries. Finally, we manually revised all the automatically produced alignments by the tool. Although a considerable part of the alignments were correct, we still had to apply manual corrections on about 2,000 alignments. As result, we obtained 13,847 pairs of correctly aligned French-Spanish sentences. This is the gold data for the evaluation.

Once we have the reference alignments ready, we align the sentences based on two previous methods. For that, we utilize the Hunalign software. This tool can perform the work based only on sentence length information (6). In this case, the input data is the pair of texts to be aligned. This first method produces our baseline alignments. In addition, the software can also align sentences based on the combination of sentence length and bilingual dictionary information. In this case, the input data is the same pair of texts and a good bilingual dictionary. This second method is supposed to produce better results than the baseline.

Finally, we are ready to evaluate our algorithm. It receives as input the 14,941 non-lemmatized English sentences coming from the English-French corpus and the 14,356 non-lemmatized English sentences coming from the English-Spanish corpus. Initially, it produces 14,855 non-validated English-English sentence alignments. We call it non-validated because at this point our algorithm still needs to confirm whether every pair of aligned English sentences matches exactly the same string of characters for both corpora. After the validation process has taken place, it produces a total amount of 13,711 English-English sentence alignments in the clean ladder alignment history.

## 4 Results and Discussions

First, we want to check the performance of the alignment based only on sentence length information, which is our baseline. For this, we provide the Hunalign tool with 14,941 lemmatized sentences from the French corpus and the 14,356 lemmatized sentences from the Spanish corpus. Consequently, it produces 13,459 true positives out of 13,847 and 1,354 false positives. This outcome indicates a precision rate of 0.908. The number of false negatives is 388 (13,847-13,459), resulting on a recall rate of 0.972. Table 1 shows these results under the column Baseline.

Second, we want to check the performance of the alignment based on sentence length combined with bilingual dictionary information. Now, the tool receives as input the same lemmatized parallel corpus and our French-Spanish bilingual dictionary having 69,231 entries. It produces 13,704 true positives out of 13,847, while the number of false positives is 1,146. As for the precision rate, it raises to 0.923. The number of false negatives decreases to 143 (13,847-13,704) cases, producing a recall rate of 0.989. The results of this experiment are summarized on the SL+Dic column of Table 1.

Third, after obtaining the 13,711 sentence pairs described in the last paragraph of Section 3, our algorithm removes the null sentence pairs and those having null translations. Finally we obtain a French-Spanish parallel corpus having 13,640 entries. Then we compare our alignments with the reference. On the one hand, we obtain a result of 13,542 correct alignments and 98 incorrect ones. In other words, the number of true positives is 13,542 instances while the number of false positives is just 98 cases. This result indicates a very good precision rate of 0.993. On the other hand, the algorithm misses 305 (13,847-13,542) alignments that are still possible. This figure represents the instances of false negatives, which leads to a recall rate of 0.978. Table 1 contains these results under its last column.

For this particular data, the misses of correct alignments is more than 3 times the number of false positives, representing a loss rate of 2.2% of all possible correct alignments. This implies that if the size of a parallel corpus for training a statistical machine translator model is very large, the loss would be irrelevant since the amount of training data would still be very large. For such a purpose and under such conditions, an excellent precision rate is much more relevant than a perfect recall. Note that the highest possible precision rate is essential because otherwise wrong sentence alignments necessarily produce wrong word misalignments and consequently wrong translations. However when the number of wrong sentence alignments present in the parallel corpora is minimal (i.e. less than 1%), lesser will be the errors introduced to the posterior training of word alignments. In fact, good translation models depend not only on the size of a parallel corpus, but also on the high quality of the sentence alignments. In Table 1, we present the results of the evaluation by using three methods: 1) sentence length (SL) information (baseline), 2) sentence length + bilingual dictionary (SL+Dic) information and 3) our method, which is based on the high quality of existing alignments with the pivot language. Note also that the method proposed by Gale and Church, 1991 is indicated as a baseline when there is no other source of information available than the sentences themselves. However, when a good bilingual dictionary is available, an improvement is observed and the precision rate rises in 15% = (100-(1,146*100/1,354))/100 for the tested data. But an even better result is obtained when a high quality alignment has been previously performed with a pivot language. The improvement we could observe from applying our method was 92% = (100-(98*100/1,354))/100 for the tested data. This excellent result suggests that our method is efficient to transfer the original alignment information from a pair of parallel corpora sharing a common language to aligning the new pair of languages in question.

| | Baseline | SL+Dic | Our method |
|---|---|---|---|
| True positives | 13,459 | 13,704 | 13,542 |
| False positives | 1,354 | 1,146 | 98 |
| False negatives | 388 | 143 | 305 |
| Precision | 0.908 | 0.923 | *0.993* |
| Recall | 0.972 | 0.989 | 0.978 |

Table 1: French-Spanish sentence alignment using three methods

## 4 Conclusions and Future Work

A number of natural language processing applications heavily depend upon the availability of a parallel corpus. Statistical machine translation for instance requires a parallel corpus containing a huge amount of aligned sentence pairs in both languages. However, the lack of availability of almost perfectly aligned non-English parallel corpus makes unfeasible the development of such applications and researches.

Nevertheless, the relatively recent availability of the Europarl corpus which aligns English sentences with other 20 European languages has shed light on the development of our new method for obtaining such a training data. We have introduced a technique, which allows for sentence alignments of non-English texts based on the original English alignments, given a multilingual parallel corpus such as the Europarl.

Our method has been evaluated and tested against two previous methods: the first one utilizing sentence length information (baseline), while the second one, combining sentence length with bilingual dictionary information. Our method has proved to be much more efficient to align French and Spanish sentences than the other two previous methods. By applying our method, we could observe an error rate reduction of false positives of 92% in comparison with the baseline. Of course, this is due to the good quality of the original alignments, which are present in the Europarl corpus. Unfortunately, the proposed approach of aligning corpora at the sentence level cannot be applied to all sorts of bilingual data as it needs the source and target already aligned with a pivot language. This is a limitation of course, but even more limiting is when there is no reliable parallel corpus available at all for the desired language pairs.

Further work on this area stands for applying our method over all the 20 European languages of the Europarl texts. The use of our method will allow for building up to 190 new language pairs out of these corpora. We intend to develop mechanisms to process all this data and make the non-English parallel corpora available for future research and development of natural language processing applications. We hope this contribution will foster research and innovation in order to help on the development of machine translation systems for language pairs which data is not affordable or cannot be easily obtained.

## Acknowledgments

This scientific work has been financed by the Prometeo Project of the Secretaría de Educación Superior de Ciencia, Tecnología e Innovación, SENESCYT of the Republic of Ecuador under the grant 20130943. We also would like to thank researcher Philipp Koehn who contributed by providing valuable information for validating the novelty of this research.

## References

Brown, P.F. et al.: A Statistical Approach to Machine Translation. Computational Linguistics, 16(2), 79-85 (1990).

Davis, M., Dunning T.: A TREC Evaluation of Query Translation Methods for Multi-Lingual Text Retrieval. Fourth Text Retrieval Conference (TREC-4). NIST (1995).

Eisele, A., Chen, Y.: MultiUN: A Multilingual Corpus from United Nation Documents. Proceedings of the Seventh conference on International Language Resources and Evaluation, Pages 2868-2872, La Valletta, Malta, European Language Resources Association (ELRA), 5/2010, www.dfki.de/lt/publication_show.php?id=4790.

ELRA: SCI-FRES-EURADIC French-Spanish Bilingual Dictionary. Catalog Reference : ELRA-M0035, http://catalog.elra.info/product_info.php?cPath

=42_45&products_id=668.

EU Official Journal Multilingual Legal Text in 22 European Languages, http://apertium.eu/data

Gale, W.A., Church, K. W.: Identifying Word Correspondences in Parallel Texts. Fourth DARPA Workshop on Speech and Natural language, Asilomar, California (1991).

Gale, W.A., Church, K. W.: A Program for Aligning Sentences in Bilingual Corpora. Computational Linguistics, 19(1) (1993).

Koehn, P.: Europarl: A Parallel Corpus for Statistical Machine Translation, MT Summit (2005), www.statmt.org/europarl/

Landauer, T.K., Littman, M. L.: Fully Automatic Cross-Language Document Retrieval Using Latent Semantic Indexing. Proceedings of the Sixth Annual Conference of the UW Centre for the New Oxford English Dictionary and Text Research, pp. 31-38, UW Centre for the New OED and Text Research, Waterloo, Ontario (1990)

Melamed, I.D.: Word-to-word Models of Translation Equivalence. IRCS technical report #98-08, University of Pennsylvania (1998)

Melamed, I.D.: Automatic Discovery of Noncompositional Compounds in Parallel Data. Proceedings of the 2nd Conference on Empirical Methods in Natural Language Processing (EMNLP-97), Brown University (1997).

Oard, D.W.: Cross-language Text Retrieval Research in the USA. Third DELOS Workshop. European Research Consortium for Informatics and Mathematics (1997).

Ralf, S. et al. : The JRC-Acquis: A Multilingual Aligned Parallel Corpus with 20+ Languages. Proceedings of the 5th International Conference on Language Resources and Evaluation (LREC'2006). Genoa, Italy, (2006), http://ipsc.jrc.ec.europa.eu/index.php?id=198.

Schmid, H.: Probabilistic Part-of-Speech Tagging Using Decision Trees. Proceedings of International Conference on New Methods in Language Processing, Manchester, UK, 1994. www.cis.unimuenchen.de/~schmid/tools/Tree Tagger/.

Tiedemann, J.: News from OPUS - A Collection of Multilingual Parallel Corpora with Tools and Interfaces. Recent Advances in Natural Language Processing (vol V), pages 237-248, John Benjamins, Amsterdam/Philadelphia (2009), http://opus.lingfil.uu.se/ECB.php

Varga, D. et al. : Parallel Corpora for Medium Density Languages. In Proceedings of the RANLP 2005, pages 590-596 (2005)

# Language Technologies for Suicide Prevention in Social Media

José M. Gómez
Department of Software and Computing Systems, University of Alicante
jmgomez@ua.es

Abstract

At present, the suicide phenomenon is raising, having a relevant impact on our society. Each year about one million people die as a result of suicidal behavior becoming an economic, social and human problem. On the other hand, the use of Social Media as a means of communication is becoming extremely popular, through which their emotional states and impressions are exchanged. Therefore, it is no surprise that more and more people with depression publish their suicide notes in these communication channels. In this context, Information Technologies and Communications and, more specifically, Language Technologies play an important role in the early detection of the depression, their causes and their terrible consequences. Based on these considerations, it is mandatory to provide societal, environmentally approaches and solutions to tackle these societal challenges. This work pretends to be an exhaustive survey of the different researches in this scope, in order to explain which methodologies, technologies and resources are used in the detection of mental problems by means of the Social Media analysis as well as to reveal their deficiencies.

## 1 Introduction

In Europe, suicide has become the leading cause of violent death (WHO, 2014). Each year 804.000 people die in the world as a result of suicidal behaviour and the number of attempts is about 20 times higher (WHO, 2012; WHO, 2014). It is estimated that in 2020, about 1.53 million people will die as a result of suicidal acts. Preventing suicide is one of the five areas of priority of the European Pact for Mental Health and Well-Being[1], which was launched by the European Commission in 2008. Suicide is the third leading cause of violent death among people aged 15 to 44, followed by accidents and homicides (Holmes et al., 2007), and it would be the second reason that would explain the deaths in the group of people aged 15 to 19 years (WHO, 2014). Suicidal behavior can be defined as a complex process that can range from suicidal ideation (communicated through verbal or non-verbal means) to planning of suicide, attempting suicide, and in the worst case, the suicide itself. These behaviors are influenced by interacting biological, genetic, psychological, social, environmental and situational factors (Wasserman et al., 2004).

Suicide has also been strong linked to inequity, social exclusion and socio-economic deprivation (Berk and Dodd, 2006). It is an enormous problem that causing unnecessary human suffering and immeasurable costs for society. According to Josee Van Remoortel, advisor to the European organization Mental Health Europe[2] (MHE), the financial crisis is affecting "all areas of life", not just economies, and its impact on mental health is creating a "deep chasm in our society".

## 2 Internet and Social Media Penetration

In the other hand, studies reveal that between 90.1% and 97.8% of young people between 10 and

-------------

[1]http://ec.europa.eu/health/ph_determinants/life_style/mental/docs/pact_en.pdf
[2]http://www.mhe-sme.org/

15 years, access the Internet[3]; and, around 88.5% of youth, aged 16 to 24 choose social networks as a way to communicate. Therefore, the use of this type of technology can be up to 90.2%, in the case of students (García-Rabagó et al., 2010). Forums, chats, social networks, blogs, micro-blogs or e-mails are virtual spaces where Internet users can interact freely and even fantasize, using anonymous identities. This implies that people with suicidal tendencies, tend to express their thoughts, desires and intentions in pro-suicide forums and share with other people, feelings and intentions (Moreno Gea and Blanco Sanchez, 2012).

They also warn their suicidal intentions through the Web in real time, be-fore and while committing the act (Sarno, 2008). The study conducted in (Mingote et al., 2004) also proves that the younger are one of the population segments where prevention is particularly necessary, finding that 20% of suicides occur among adolescents and young adults.

## 3 Suicide Prevention in Social Media

It is important to raise awareness on that most self-inflicted deaths are potentially preventable. Well-known studies concerning research on suicide (Owen et al., 2012; Isometsa, 2001; Cantor, 2000; Rudestam, 1971) show that a high number of people who decide to end with their lives. Through suicide had no prior contact with mental health services, but had communicated their suicidal plans or thoughts directly or indirectly through different means to members of their family, friends, colleagues or through their social networks. Improve the staff skills in early recognition of suicide warning signs, is an essential issue to prevent suicidal mortality. There is an increasing tendency (Ruder et al., 2011) where suicide notes are posted on the social media (e.g., Facebook, Twitter), where Internet users (and not necessarily teenagers) announce their suicidal thoughts before committing suicide. This poses new challenges for human language technologies since, traditional existing automatic tools are not able to process the new language employed in the social media (abbreviations, slang, smiles and, more generally, a low unstructured and highly informal language).

The Internet, and specifically the Web 2.0, is an important source of information for learning about suicidal behaviors (Dunlop et al., 2011). The way individuals respond to help request from people at high risk of suicide or interact with them can lead to the fact that the potential suicidal may reconsider his/her final decision, or, on the contrary, encourage and accelerate the process of ending with his/her life (Wasserman et al., 2004).

During the recent years, some popular social networks, such as Facebook have become the most important means of social communication, with nearly 1,230 million of registered users world-wide[4], 70% of whom are young people who make frequent use of this type of media, through which the emotional states and impressions are exchanged (Dunlop et al., 2011; Lenhart et al., 2010). These social networks are also a way to find comfort and welfare and its usage promotes contact and positive support among young people, especially among those with mental disorders (Ellison et al., 2007). In addition, the Web offers possibilities for early detection on suicidal behaviors and it may constitute a cost-effective means of intervention based on a first step care approach. Their use may be of help for identifying pro-suicide messages, detecting group pat-terns, analyzing exposure to the warning signs and intervening in a personalized manner with people at risk who are willing to accept professional help. In order to raise awareness of the ways people could get help when showing a suicidal behavior, Facebook and the Samaritans[5] association developed a joint initiative consisting in adding a new feature to Facebook, where anyone worried about a friend could fill out a form, detailing

[3]http://ec.europa.eu/eurostat/product?code=isoc_pibi_use&mode=view

[4]http://investor.fb.com/releasedetail.cfm?ReleaseID=821954

[5]http://www.samaritans.org/

related to suicide prevention. With the development of Web 2.0 new forms of communication arise that allow to interactively disseminate information through forums, blogs, micro-blogs, mobile apps, etc. These technologies provide new opportunities to define and develop suicide prevention strategies. The use of e-health technologies has many beneficial applications for society. Every day millions of people access the Web to find, provide and share information about opinions, feelings and even plans and intentions. Recognizing suicidal warning signs will be the first necessary step to help and offer support to these people. A study that examines the warning signs of suicide on the Internet (Mandrusiak et al., 2006) found that the searches with the terms "warning signals" and "suicide" produced approximately 183,000 outcomes. Warning signs could be categorized in terms of cognitive content, behavioral, situational or other indicators concerning psychological characteristics or interpersonal problems. They could identify suicidal groups that need urgent intervention. Internet searches for suicide may pro-vide a faster way of monitoring possible trends in suicide.

Some clinical studies observed that de-pressed patients frequently speech slow, uniform, monotonous and with a low voice (Kuny and Stassen, 1993) or to have psychomotor symptoms and this is reflected in the speech (Sobin and Sackeim, 1997). Moreover, emotions and mood can influence the speaking behavior of a person and the characteristics of the sound in speech (Kuny and Stassen, 1993; Bachorowski and Owren, 1995; Sobin and Alpert, 1999; Scherer, 2003; Goudbeek and Scherer, 2010). The speech of depressed patients is characterized by a longer pause duration, that is, an increased amount of time between speech utterances as well as by a reduced variability in mean vocal pitch (Lamers et al., 2014). For these reasons, the acoustic speech features can be used to build models and algorithms for automated depression detection in clinical scenarios.

But these acoustic features are not the only ones that can be used, Internet usage itself (Katikala-pudi et al., 2012), social networking behaviors (Moreno et al., 2011; Choudhury et al., 2012) or location sharing (Park et al., 2013) can vary as a function of being depressed. (Quercia et al., 2012) found correlations between sentiment and levels of popularity, influence and general well-being using the network relations among users and (O'Connor et al., 2010) used a measure of public opinion. All these methods can be applied to analyze emotion in suicide notes (Liakata et al., 2012).

## 5 Human Language Technologies and Suicide Prevention

In order to resolve this social issue, Language Technologies (LT) could help with the early identification of "suicide warning signs" that will be useful to detect individuals with suicidal ideation, as well as virtual environments where pro-suicide information is being shared or suicidal attempts are being encouraged. In particular, LT can analyze language structures and their meaning (Navigli, 2009) on different textual genres. Tasks such as information retrieval (Salton and McGill, 1986), information extraction (Cowie and Lehnert, 1996), text classification and clustering (Sebastiani, 2002), or sentiment analysis (Pang and Lee, 2008) are basic pillars of these technologies that allow the construction of more complex automatic processes for discovering knowledge from oral and/or written text.

Recent research in LT has been proved great potential in the area of healthcare. From the development of applications to assist medical practitioners in the access and management of information about patients, e.g. (Iakovidis and Smailis, 2012; Vest, 2012), to the creation of computer programs to support and/or facilitate reading comprehension for language-impaired children during communication (Dietz et al., 2011; Wang and Paul, 2011). So far, and to the best of our knowledge, very little effort has been made to apply LT for the benefit of suicide prevention.

The linguistic analysis of suicide notes has a long history and already started as early as 1956 with the work of (Shneidman and Farberow, 1956), followed by several others (Osgood and Walker, 1959; Gleser et al., 1961; Edelman and Renshaw, 1982). The basis of most of this research was a corpus of 66 suicides notes, half genuine and half simulated, collected by Schneidman and the task was to identify those textual features which could differentiate between genuine and fake notes. Whereas the earlier work mostly focused on the manual analysis and detection of these differentiating features, e.g. by relying on techniques from discourse analysis (Shneidman and Farberow, 1956) or by focusing on shallow text characteristics such as the usage of modals and auxiliaries (Osgood and Walker, 1959), the choice of verbs and adverbs (Gleser et al., 1961), etc. We can observe a recent tendency to also rely on automatic corpus analysis techniques for the automatic detection of suicide messages. (Shapero, 2011), for example, studied two corpora of suicide notes in an attempt to define the typical suicide note. For doing so, she automatically calculated word usage and semantic concepts in the notes. (Pennebaker and Chung, 2011) used the frequency of verbal elements in a narrative that express a certain mood or sentiment which show that there is also ample evidence that text mining techniques based on the frequency of certain terms can be applied to narratives from patients in order to monitor changes in mood. As far as we know, (Pestian et al., 2010) were the first to experiment with the use machine learning techniques for the automatic classification of suicide notes. In experiments on the earlier described data set of 66 notes, they investigated whether a machine learning system was able to classify suicide notes with a higher accuracy than mental health professionals. They showed that the best machine learners were indeed able to outperform the human experts. More recent studies confirm this fact (Janssen et al., 2013), underlining once again the added value of automated speech analysis. (Howes et al., 2014) present an initial investigation into the application of computational linguistic techniques, such as topic and sentiment modelling, to online therapy for depression and anxiety using Latent Dirichlet Allocation (Blei et al., 2003). However, early works tried to detect specific emotions such as anger, surprise, fear, etc. using dictionary-based or machine-learning-based approaches (Chuang and Wu, 2004; Seol et al., 2008) and more recently (Purver and Battersby, 2012; Choudhury et al., 2012; Neuman et al., 2012; Howes et al., 2014).

Although interesting research was conducted on the Schneidman data set, the focus should not be on distinguishing between genuine and elicited suicide notes. Instead, it is of key importance to determine what exactly makes a note a real suicide note, independently of the features of the elicited notes or the distinguishing characteristics between both types of notes. Such a suicide note corpus of positive-only data, annotated with fine-grained emotions, was released in the framework of the 2011 i2b2 Natural Language Processing Challenge (Pestian et al., 2012) on emotion classification in suicide notes. Although the scope of the challenge (differentiating between emotions in positive-only data) was different, it led to the creation of a permanently available resource facilitating future research in emotion detection in suicide notes. The corpus contains the notes writ-ten by 1319 people, before they committed suicide. The notes were collected between 1950 and 2011. Spelling and grammar errors were kept in the data. All notes were anonymized by replacing all names with other values and by randomly shifting dates within the same year. The data set of the challenge consisted of a training set of 600 suicide notes, and a test set of 300 notes. The challenge itself revealed that not only shallow lexical, but also semantic features contributed to classification performance. However, many challenges remain to be investigated: the sensitivity of the current systems to spelling and other errors -especially in online data-, the lack of deep understanding of the data through the use of mainly shallow features, etc. The release of this data set has made it possible to accurately detect and differentiate between different emotions, which might be indicative of suicidal behavior.

For the automatic detection and classification of emotions in suicidal content, we can rely on the recent advances in the domain of LT (Jurafsky and Martin, 2008) and machine learning (Mitchell, 1997). Whereas the international LT research community until recently mainly focused on the "factual" aspects of content analysis, we can observe an additional growing interest in the analysis of attitude and affect in textual sources, especially in online content such as blogs, tweets, social network data, etc. The extraction of affective contents does not only imply the detection of opinions, evaluations, beliefs and speculations in text (topics which have a high application potential in customer intelligence applications and the like), but also the identification of certain emo-tions. For example, how do people express their intent to commit suicide? The use of machine learning techniques and sentiment analysis techniques for the automatic analysis of suicide notes is not new. (Huang et al., 2007), for example, experimented with lexicon-based sentiment analysis for the automatic detection of suicidal blogs. (Pes-tian et al., 2010) combined shallow text characteristics, such as part-of-speech information, readability scores and parse information with the machine learning software as available in the Weka package.

Until we know, the most complete research about suicide prevention in the social networks, specifically Facebook, is the work of (Schwartz et al., 2014). However, instead of trying to detect suicide notes or to differentiate people with or without mental disorders, they measure the changes across time of the degree of depression.

## 6 Conclusions

The magnitude of the suicide in the EU member states and the rest of the world make suicide prevention not exclusively a problem of Mental Health. This is a problem that must be addressed from a multidisciplinary perspective, involving different areas. Internet Technologies and Communication and, more specifically, the Human Language Technologies can help to resolve part of these problems through the early detection of suicidal thoughts and/or behavior expressed through the Social Media. The words and the way people use to communicate in their blogs, social networks, etc. provide information about the psychological state and personality of individuals. The processing and analysis of natural language texts shared via Internet helps record and detect changes in cognitive and emotional state of the people. Unfortunately, although there are avail-able resources and tools for sentiment analysis and opinion mining, even in the field of the depression detection and using different approaches and features, there is neither system nor platform that deal with the full process of suicide prevention.

## Acknowledgements

This research work has been partially funded by the Spanish Government and the European Commission through the project, ATTOS (TIN2012-38536-C03- 03), LEGOLANG (TIN2012-31224), SAM (FP7- 611312) and FIRST (FP7-287607).

## References

Jo-Anne Bachorowski and Michael J. Owren. 1995. VOCAL EXPRESSION OF EMOTION:. Acoustic Properties of Speech Are Associated With Emotional Intensity and Context. Psychological Science, 6(4):219–224, July.

Barr, D. Taylor-Robinson, A. Scott-Samuel, M. McKee, and D Stuckler. 2012. Suicides associated with the 2008-10 economic recession in England: time trend analysis. British Medical Journal, 345:1–7.

M. Berk and Henry S. Dodd. 2006. The effect of

macroeconomic variables on suicide. Psychol Med, 36(2):181–189.

David M. Blei, Andrew Y. Ng, and Michael I. Jordan. 2003. Latent dirichlet allocation. The Journal of Machine Learning Research, 3:993–1022, March.

Christopher H. Cantor. 2000. The International Handbook of Suicide and Attempted Suicide. In Keith Hawton and Kees van Heeringen, editors, The Inter-national Handbook of Suicide and Attempted Suicide. John Wiley & Sons, Ltd, West Sussex, Enland, January.

Munmun De Choudhury, Michael Gamon, and Scott Counts. 2012. Happy, Nervous or Surprised? Classification of Human Affective States in Social Me-dia. In ICWSM, Dublin, Ireland.

Ze-Jing Chuang and Chung-Hsien Wu. 2004. Multi-Modal Emotion Recognition from Speech and Text.

International Journal of Computational Linguistics & Chinese Language Processing, Volume 9, Number 2, August 2004: Special Issue on New Trends of Speech and Language Processing, 9(2):45–62.

Jim Cowie and Wendy Lehnert. 1996. Information extraction. Communications of the ACM, 39(1):80–91, January.

A Dietz, A Ball, and J Griffith. 2011. Reading and writing with aphasia in the 21st century: technological applications of supported reading comprehension and written expression. Top Stroke Rehabil, 18(6):758–769.

S.M. Dunlop, E. More, and D. Romer. 2011. Where do youth learn about suicide on the internet, and what influence does this have on suicidal ideation?

The Journal of Child Psychology and Psychiatry, 52(10):1073–1080.

A.M. Edelman and S L Renshaw. 1982. Genuine versus simulated suicide notes: an issue revisited through discourse analysis. Suicide & life-threatening behavior, 12(2):103–13, January.

N.B. Ellison, C. Steinfield, and C. Lampe. 2007. The benefits of Facebbok friend's: Social capital and college students' use of online social network sites. Journal of Computer-Mediated Communication, 12:1143–1168.

Horacio Garcıa-Rabago, Jose E Sahagun-Flores, Alfonso Ruiz-Gomez, Gustavo M Sanchez Urena, Juan C Tirado-Vargas, and Jaime G Gonzalez-Gamez. 2010. Comparing high- and low-lethality factors regarding attempted suicide-associated risk factors. Revista de salud publica (Bogota, Colombia), 12(5):713–21, October.

G. C. Gleser, L. A. Gottschalk, and K. J. Springer. 1961. An anxiety scale applicable to verbal samples.

Archives of general psychiatry, 5:593–605, December.

Martijn Goudbeek and Klaus Scherer. 2010. Be-yond arousal: valence and potency/control cues in the vocal expression of emotion. The Journal of the Acoustical Society of America, 128(3):1322–36, September.

Emily A. Holmes, Catherine Crane, Melanie J. V. Fen-nell, and J.Mark G. Williams. 2007. Imagery about suicide in depression-"flash-forwards"? Journal of Behavior Therapy and Experimental Psychiatry, 38:423–434.

Christine Howes, Matthew Purver, and Rose McCabe. 2014. Linguistic Indicators of Severity and Progress in Online Text-based Therapy for Depression. In

Proceedings of the Workshop on Computational Linguistics and Clinical Psychology: From Linguistic Signal to Clinical Reality, pages 7–16, Baltimore. Association for Computational Linguistics.

Yen-Pei Huang, Tiong Goh, and Chern Li Liew. 2007. Hunting Suicide Notes in Web 2.0 - Preliminary Findings. In Ninth IEEE International Symposium on Multimedia Workshops (ISMW 2007), pages 517– 521. IEEE, December.

D Iakovidis and C Smailis. 2012. A semantic model for multimodal data mining in healthcare information systems. Stud Health Technol Inform, 180:574– 578.

E T Isometsa.¨ 2001. Psychological autopsy studies–

a review. European psychiatry : the journal of the Association of European Psychiatrists, 16(7):379–85, November.

Joris H. Janssen, Paul Tacken, J.J.G. (Gert-Jan) de Vries, Egon L. van den Broek, Joyce H.D.M. Westerink, Pim Haselager, and Wijnand A. IJsselsteijn. 2013. Machines Outperform Laypersons in Recognizing Emotions Elicited by Autobiographical Recollection. Human–Computer Interaction, 28(6):479–517, November.

Daniel Jurafsky and James H. Martin. 2008. Speech and Language Processing, 2nd Edition.

Raghavendra Katikalapudi, Sriram Chellappan, Frances Montgomery, Donald Wunsch, and Karl Lutzen. 2012. Associating Internet Usage with Depressive Behavior Among College Students. IEEE Technology and Society Magazine, 31(4):73–80.

S Kuny and H H Stassen. 1993. Speaking behav-ior and voice sound characteristics in depressive patients during recovery. Journal of psychiatric research, 27(3):289–307.

Sanne M.A. Lamers, Khiet P. Truong, Bas Steunenberg, Franciska de Jong, and Gerben J. Westerhof. 2014. Applying prosodic speech features in mental health care: An exploratory study in a life-review intervention for depression. In Proceedings of the Workshop on Computational Linguistics and Clinical Psychology: From Linguistic Signal to Clinical Reality, pages 61–68, Baltimore. Association for Computational Linguistics.

Amanda Lenhart, Kristen Purcell, Aaron Smith, and Kathryn Zickuhr. 2010. Social Media & Mobile Internet Use Among Teens and Young Adults. Techni-cal report, Pew Research Center, Washington, D.C.

Maria Liakata, Jee-Hyub Kim, Shyamasree Saha, Janna Hastings, and Dietrich Rebholz-Schuhmann. 2012. Three hybrid classifiers for the detection of emotions in suicide notes. Biomedical informatics insights, 5(Suppl. 1):175–84, January.

Michael Mandrusiak, M David Rudd, Thomas E Joiner, Alan L Berman, Kimberly A Van Orden, and Tracy Witte. 2006. Warning signs for suicide on the Inter-net: a descriptive study. Suicide & life-threatening behavior, 36(3):263–71, June.

J.C Mingote, M.A Jimenez,´ R Osorio, and T. Palomo. 2004. Suicidio. Asistencia Cl´ınica. In Gu´ıa de practica´ medica´, chapter 4, pages 19–30. D´ıaz San-tos.

Thomas M. Mitchell. 1997. Machine Learning. McGraw-Hill, Inc., New York, NY, USA, March.

Megan A Moreno, Lauren A Jelenchick, Katie G Egan, Elizabeth Cox, Henry Young, Kerry E Gannon, and Tara Becker. 2011. Feeling bad on Face-book: depression disclosures by college students on a social networking site. Depression and anxiety, 28(6):447–55, June.

Pedro Moreno Gea and Carmen Blanco Sanchez´. 2012. Suicidio e Internet. Medidas preventivas y de ac-tuacion´. Psiquiatria.com, 16.

Navigli. 2009. Word Sense Disambiguation: A Survey. ACM Computing Surveys, 41(2).

Yair Neuman, Yohai Cohen, Dan Assaf, and Gabbi Kedma. 2012. Proactive screening for depres-sion through metaphorical and automatic text analy-sis. Artificial intelligence in medicine, 56(1):19–25, September.

Brendan O'Connor, Ramnath Balasubramanyan, Bryan R. Routledge, and Noah A. Smith. 2010. From Tweets to Polls : Linking Text Sentiment to Public Opinion Time Series. In Fourth International AAAI Conference on Weblogs and Social Media.

C. E. Osgood and E. G. Walker. 1959. Motivation and language behavior: a content analysis of suicide notes. Journal of abnormal psychology, 59(1):58–67, July.

Gareth Owen, Judith Belam, Helen Lambert, Jenny Donovan, Frances Rapport, and Christabel Owens. 2012. Suicide communication events: lay interpretation of the communication of suicidal ideation and intent. Social science & medicine (1982), 75(2):419–28, July.

Bo Pang and Lillian Lee. 2008. Opinion Mining and Sentiment Analysis. Foundations and Trends R in Information Retrieval, 2(1–2):1–135, January.

Sungkyu Park, Sang Won Lee, Jinah Kwak,

Meeyoung Cha, and Bumseok Jeong. 2013. Activities on Face-book reveal the depressive state of users. Journal of medical Internet research, 15(10):e217, January.

James W. Pennebaker and Cindy K. Chung. 2011. Expressive Writing, Emotional Upheavals, and Health. In Howard S. Friedman, editor, Expressive Writing, Emotional Upheavals, and Health, chapter 18, page
936. Oxford University Press.

J. Pestian, H. Nasrallah, Matykiewicz, A. Bennett, and A. Leenaars. 2010. Suicide Note Classification Us-ing Natural Language Processing. Biomed Inform Insights, 3:19–28.

John P Pestian, Pawel Matykiewicz, Michelle Linn-Gust, Brett South, Ozlem Uzuner, Jan Wiebe, K Bre-tonnel Cohen, John Hurdle, and Christopher Brew. 2012. Sentiment Analysis of Suicide Notes: A Shared Task. Biomedical informatics insights, 5(Suppl 1):3–16, January.

Matthew Purver and Stuart Battersby. 2012. Experimenting with distant supervision for emotion classi-fication. In 13th Conference of the European Chap-ter of the Association for Computational Linguistics (EACL), pages 482–491. Association for Computa-tional Linguistics, Stroudsburg, PA, USA, April.

Daniele Quercia, Jonathan Ellis, Licia Capra, and Jon Crowcroft. 2012. Tracking "gross community happiness" from tweets. In Proceedings of the ACM 2012 conference on Computer Supported Cooperative Work - CSCW '12, page 965, New York, New York, USA, February. ACM Press.

Thomas D Ruder, Gary M Hatch, Garyfalia Ampanozi, Michael J Thali, and Nadja Fischer. 2011. Suicide announcement on Facebook. Crisis, 32(5):280–2, January.

Kjell E. Rudestam. 1971. Stockholm and Los Angeles: A cross-cultural study of the communication of suicidal intent. Journal of Consulting and Clinical Psychology, 36(1):82–90.

Gerard Salton and Michael J. McGill. 1986. Introduction to Modern Information Retrieval. McGraw-Hill, Inc., New York, NY, USA.

David Sarno. 2008. Rise and fall of the Googled swastika.

K Scherer. 2003. Vocal communication of emotion: A review of research paradigms. Speech Communication, 40(1-2):227–256, April.

H. Andrew Schwartz, Johannes Eichstaedt, Margaret L. Kern, Gregory Park, Maarten Sap, David Stillwell, Michal Kosinski, and Lyle Ungar. 2014. Towards Assessing Changes in Degree of Depression through Facebook. In Proceedings of the Workshop on Computational Linguistics and Clinical Psychology: From Linguistic Signal to Clinical Reality, pages 118–125, Baltimore. Association for Computational Linguistics.

Fabrizio Sebastiani. 2002. Machine learning in automated text categorization. ACM Computing Surveys, 34(1):1–47, March.

Young-Soo Seol, Dong-Joo Kim, and Han-Woo Kim.
2008. Emotion Recognition from Text Using Knowledge-based ANN. Proceedings of ITC-CSCC, 9(2).

Jess Jann Shapero. 2011. The language of suicide notes, July.

E. S. Shneidman and N. L. Farberow. 1956. Clues to suicide. Public health reports, 71(2):109–14, Febru-ary.

C Sobin and M Alpert. 1999. Emotion in speech: the acoustic attributes of fear, anger, sadness, and joy. Journal of psycholinguistic research, 28(4):347–65, July.

C Sobin and H A Sackeim. 1997. Psychomotor symptoms of depression. The American journal of psychiatry, 154(1):4–17, January.

P Sobocki, I Lekander, and F Borgstrom¨. 2007. The economic burden of depression in Sweden from 1997 to 2005. Eur Psychiatry, 22(3):146–152.

David Stuckler, Sanjay BasuMarc, Adam Coutts Suhrcke, and McKee. Martin. 2011. Effects of the 2008 recession on health: a first look at European data. The Lancet, 378(9786):124 – 125.

JR Vest. 2012. Health information exchange: national and international approaches. Adv Health Care Manag, 12:3–24.

Y Wang and P.V. Paul. 2011. Integrating technology and reading instruction with children who are deaf or hard of hearing: the effectiveness of the Cornerstones project. Am Ann Deaf, 156(1):56–68.

Danuta Wasserman, Ellenor Mittendorfer Rutz, Wolfgang Rutz, and Armin Schmidtke. 2004. Suicide Prevention In Europe. Technical report, National and Stockholm County Council's Centre for Suicide Research and Prevention of Mental Ill-Health.

WHO. 2012. Public health action for the prevention of suicide: a framework. Technical report, World Health Organization.

WHO. 2014. Preventing suicide: A global imperative. Technical report, World Health Organization.

# A Supervised Approach for Sentiment Analysis using Skipgrams

Javi Fernández, José M. Gómez, Patricio Martínez-Barco Department of Software and Computing Systems University of Alicante
{javifm,jmgomez,patricio}@dlsi.ua.es

Abstract

We present a supervised hybrid approach for Sentiment Analysis in Twitter. A sentiment lexicon is built from a dataset, where each tweet is labelled with its overall polarity. In this work, skipgrams are used as information units (in addition to words and n-grams) to enrich the sentiment lexicon with combinations of words that are not adjacent in the text. This lexicon is employed in conjunction with machine learning techniques to create a polarity classifier. The evaluation was carried out against different datasets in English and Spanish, showing an improvement with the usage of skipgrams.

## 1 Introduction

Twitter has become one of the most popular sources of data to extract subjective information from. Here, people share aspects and opinions about their everyday life. This subjective information has a great value for general users, but mainly for brands and organisations. They can monitor their reputation by analysing the sentiment of the tweets posted about them or their competitors.

However, extracting this information accordingly in Twitter texts is a very challenging task for current Sentiment Analysis (SA) approaches. The short length of the tweets (140 characters), the informality, and the lack of context, makes sentiment detection and extraction a far harder task. In addition, the vast amount of tweets (over 500 million tweets per day[7]) complicates traditional SA systems to process this subjective information in real time. The performance of SA tools has become increasingly critical.

In this paper we describe a sentiment analysis approach, that faces some of the challenges of analysing subjective information in Twitter, but taking into account its employment in real-time applications. The remainder of this paper is structured as follows. In Section 2 we briefly describe the related work in sentiment analysis and introduce our work. In Section 3 we detail the approach we propose. The evaluation performed and its discussion is provided in Section 4. Finally, Section 5 concludes the paper, and outlines the future work.

## 2 Related work

### 2.1 Sentiment Analysis

Sentiment Analysis is the field of study that identifies and extracts subjective information from texts. Two main approaches can be followed: machine learning approaches and lexicon-based approaches (Taboada2011, Medhat2014).

Machine learning approaches treat polarity classification as a text categorisation problem. Texts are usually represented as vectors of features, and depending on the features used the system can reach better results. If a labelled training set of documents is needed, the approach is defined as supervised learning; if not, it is defined as unsupervised learning. These approaches perform very well in the domain they are trained on, but their performance

[7] https://about.twitter.com/company (November 2014)

drops when the same classifier is used in a different domain (Pang2008, Tan2009). In addition, if the number of features is big, the efficiency drops dramatically.

Lexicon-based approaches make use of dictionaries of opinionated words and phrases to discern the polarity of a text. In these approaches, each word in the dictionary is assigned a score of positivity and negativity. To detect the polarity of a text, the scores of its words are combined, and the polarity with the greatest score is chosen. These dictionaries can be generated manually, semiautomatically from an initial seed of opinionated words (Kim 2004), or automatically from a labelled dataset (Cruz 2013). The major disadvantage of the first one is the incapability to find opinion words with domain and context specific orientations, while the second one helps to solve this problem (Medhat 2014). These approaches are usually faster than machine learning ones, as the combination of scores is normally a predefined mathematical function.

## 2.2 Skipgrams

Most of the current sentiment analysis approaches employ *words*, *n-grams* and *phrases* as information units for their models, either as features for machine learning approaches, or as dictionary entries in the lexicon-based approaches. However, words and n-grams have some problems to represent the flexibility and sequentiality of human language. In the case of Twitter texts, a deeper analysis of the text is not possible or accurate because of the small size, lack of context (and sometimes lack of structure), and informality (Aranberri 2013). In order to create n-grams that can represent the flexibility and sequentiality of human language, it is necessary to go further than just adjacent words. This is the reason why we decided to use of *skipgrams* in sentiment analysis.

The use of skipgrams is a technique whereby n-grams are formed (bigrams, trigrams, etc.), but in addition to using adjacent sequences of words, it also allows some words to be *skipped* (Guthrie 2006). More generally, in a *k-skip-n-gram*, *n* determines the number of terms, and *k* the maximum number of skips allowed. In this way skipgrams are new terms that retain part of the sequentiality of the terms, but in a more flexible way than n-grams (Fernandez 2014). Note that an n-gram can be defined as a 0-skip-n-gram, a skipgram where $k=0$. For example, the sentence *"I love healthy food"* has two word level trigrams: *"I love healthy"* and *"love healthy food"*. However, there is one important trigram implied by the sentence that was not captured: *"I love food"*. The use of skipgrams allows the word *"health"* be skipped, providing the mentioned trigram.

## 3 Methodology

Our contribution consists on a hybrid approach, which creates a lexicon from a labelled dataset, and builds a polarity classifier from the dataset and the generated lexicon with machine learning techniques. We tried to avoid employing external linguistic tools, to minimise the possible propagation of external errors. The system flow can be seen in Figure 1. In the following sections we describe this flow in detail.

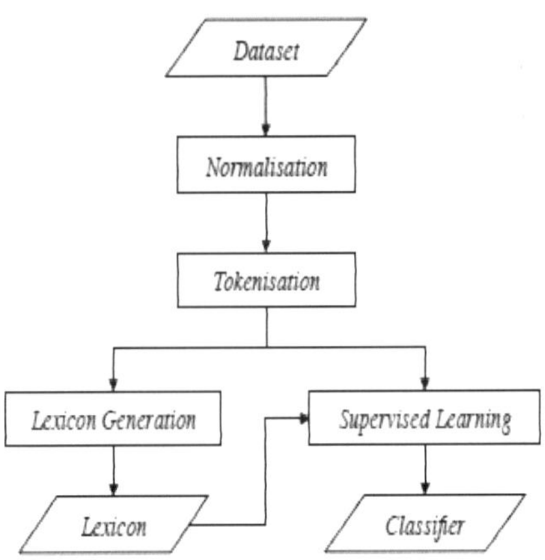


Figure 1: System flow

### 3.1 Normalisation

As we do not want to lose the subjective information given by the original text, we perform a very simple normalisation. Employing a more complex normalisation can induce some errors that would be propagated to the final results. We start converting all the tweets to lower case. Usernames and URLs are replaced by the strings *"USERNAME"* and *"URL"* respectively, as they are not words that represent subjectivity. Hashtags were not modified as they can contain some information about the topic and sentiment about the tweets.

Then, we carry out a partial character repetition removal. If the same character is repeated more than 3 times, the rest of repetitions are removed. In this way, the words are normalised, but we can still recognise if the original words had repeated characters. We do not remove all repetitions as they can be very useful to detect subjectivity in texts (Saif 2012). For example, the words *"gooood"* and *"gooooood"* would be normalised to *"goood"*, but the word *"good"* would remain the same. We assume the ambiguity of this example, which can refer to both *"good"* and *"god"*. Figure 2 shows an example of this normalisation process.

*So excited to go to #NewYork tomorrow*

*with my best friend everrrrr @John!!!!*

↓

*so excited to go to #newyork tomorrow*

*with my best friend everrrrr @john!!!!*

↓

*so excited to go to #newyork tomorrow*

*with my best friend everrr @john!!!*

↓

*so excited to go to #newyork tomorrow*

*with my best friend everrr USERNAME!!!*

Figure 2: Example of normalisation process.

## 3.2 Tokenisation

Once we have normalised the texts, we extract all the terms they contain. We consider a term as a group of adjacent characters of the same type: groups of letters, groups of numbers or groups of punctuation symbols. For example, the text *"want2go!!"* would be tokenised to the terms *"want"*, *"2"*, *"go"*, and *"!!"*. These terms are extracted using *regular expressions*. Finally, we obtain the skipgrams by making the proper combinations of the terms extracted. We show an example of this tokenisation process in Table 1.

*so excited to go to #newyork tomorrow*

*with my best friend everrr USERNAME!!!*

↓

*(so) (excited) (to) (go) (to) (#) (HASHTAG) (with)*

*(my) (best) (friend) (everrr) (USERNAME) (!!!)*

↓

*(so excited) (so to) (excited to) (excited go)*

*(to go) (to to) (go to) (go #) (to #) (to newyork)*

*(# newyork) (# tomorrow) (newyork tomorrow)*

*(newyork with) (tomorrow with) (tomorrow my)*

*(with my) (with best) (my best) (my friend)*

*(best friend) (best everrr) (friend everrr)*

*(friend USERNAME) (everrr USERNAME)*

*(everrr !!!) (USERNAME) (USERNAME !!!)*

Figure 3: Example of tokenisation process (skipgrams with $n$=2 and $k$=1)

## 3.3 Lexicon generation

Our sentiment lexicon consists on a list of skipgrams, where each skipgram has one value associated to different values of polarity, indicating how the term is related to that polarity. We called these values *polarity scores*. To build this lexicon, we need a polarity labelled dataset, which will provide both the skipgrams included in the dataset and their polarity scores. This scores depend on the number of the times the skipgram appears in text of a specific polarity, and the skips of the different occurrences. First, we explain some subscores, to understand the final formula:

- *Skip score*. This score penalises skipgrams with a high number of skipped terms. The formula applied is shown in Equation 1, where $s_i$ represents an occurrence of skipgram $s$ in the dataset, and $k_{s_i}$ is the number of skipped terms of the occurrence $s_i$.

$$skip(s_i)=\frac{1}{k_{s_i}+1} \quad (1)$$

- *Polarity ratio score*. This score indicates the proportion of texts of a specific polarity the skipgram appears in. It is calculated according the formula in Equation 2, where $p$ represents a polarity in the dataset, $S$ is the set of occurrences of the skipgram $s$ in the dataset, $S_p$ is the set of occurrences of the skipgram $s$ in texts labelled with polarity $p$. Note that this formula takes into account the skip score of the skipgram, in order to penalise skipgrams with a higher number of skipped terms.

$$ratio(s,p)=\frac{\sum_{s_i \in S_p} skip(s_i)}{|S|} \quad (2)$$

- *Polarity confidence score*. This score boosts skipgrams that appear a high number of times in texts of a specific polarity. It is calculated as shown in Equation 3.

$$confidence(s,p)=1-\frac{1}{|S_p|+1}$$

(3)

The final *polarity score* for a specific skipgram is the product of its ratio score and its confidence score. The formula employed to calculate this score can be seen in Equation 4.

$$score(s,p)=ratio(s,p)\cdot confidence(s,p) \quad (4)$$

[8] Obtained using the SemEval 2014 dataset

At the end of this process we have a list of skipgrams with a score for each polarity: our sentiment lexicon. An example of entries[8] in this lexicon can be seen in Table 1. As we can see in the example, positive words and expressions have a higher positive score, and negative words have a negative score. In addition, expressions like *happy birthday* or *good man* appear only in positive tweets, but *happy birthday* appears more times and than *good man* in the dataset, so its value is higher. Even the terms *happy* and *birthday* use to appear closer than the terms *good* and *man*, and this makes the difference much bigger.

| | Positive | Negative | Neutral |
|---|---|---|---|
| *good* | 0.799 | 0.094 | 0.101 |
| *excellent* | 0.714 | 0.000 | 0.142 |
| *happy birthday* | 0.691 | 0.000 | 0.000 |
| *good man* | 0.005 | 0.000 | 0.000 |
| *bad* | 0.258 | 0.568 | 0.155 |
| *horrible* | 0.750 | 0.000 | 0.000 |

Table 1: Example of lexicon entries.

## 3.4 Supervised learning

We use machine learning techniques to create a model able to classify the polarity of new tweets. The tweets in the dataset are employed as *training instances*, and the labelled polarities are used as *categories*. However, in contrast with text classification approaches, we employ the polarities also as *features*. The weight of each feature is calculated as specified in Equation 5, where *weight(t,p)* is the weight of polarity $p$ in the text $t$, and $S_t$ is the set of skipgrams in the text $t$.

$$weight(t,p)=\sum_{s_i \in S_t} score(s,p)\cdot skip(s_i) \quad (5)$$

Table 2 shows an example of feature weighting for the text *"I like football"* using 1-skip-2-grams[9]. Each row represents a skipgram with a value for each polarity, calculated as $score(s,p)\cdot skips(s_i)$.

[9] Obtained using the SemEval 2014 dataset

The final row is the sum of all the previous values, which will be employed as feature weights for the machine learning process.

| | Positive | Negative | Neutral |
|---|---|---|---|
| *I* | 0.422 | 0.220 | 0.356 |
| *like* | 0.354 | 0.406 | 0.235 |
| *football* | 0.346 | 0.540 | 0.102 |
| *I like* | 0.154 | 0.063 | 0.046 |
| *I football* | 0.046 | 0.037 | 0.017 |
| *like football* | 0.000 | 0.000 | 0.000 |
| weight | 1.322 | 1.266 | 0.756 |

Table 2: Example of features weights for the sentence *"I like football"* with 1-skip-2-grams

To build our model we employed *Support Vector Machines* (SVM), as it has been proved to be effective on text categorisation tasks and robust on large feature spaces (Sebastiani 2002, Mohammad 2013). More specifically, we used the *LibSVM* (Chang 2011) default implementation (*linear kernel*, $C=1$, $\varepsilon=0.1$).

## 4 Evaluation

To obtain the results of our analysis we evaluated our approach against two datasets. Both of them are divided into a *train* dataset (to create the model) and a *test* dataset (to validate the model created). The distribution of these datasets is shown in Table 3.

- *SemEval Dataset* (2013-14). This dataset was created and employed for the *Sentiment Analysis in Twitter* task in the 2013 (Nakov 2013) and 2014 (Rosenthal 2014) editions of the *SemEval*[10] workshop. It consists on 10,709 tweets in English at global level, with 3 categories: positive, negative and neutral. The neutral class covered both neutral and objective tweets. These tweets were manually annotated.
- *TASS Dataset* (2012-13). This dataset was created for the *TASS*[11] workshop, specifically for the *Sentiment Analysis* task in the 2012 edition (Villena 2013) and the *Sentiment Analysis at global level* task in 2013 (Villena 2013B). It contains 68,017 tweets in Spanish annotated at global level, with 6 categories: very positive, positive, neutral, negative, very negative and none. For our experiments we mapped these polarities into 3: positive, negative and neutral. The annotation process of these tweets was manual for the training dataset, but automatic for the test dataset, using a voting scheme from all the submissions participating in the competition.

| | **SemEval** | | **TASS** | |
|---|---|---|---|---|
| | **Train** | **Test** | **Train** | **Test** |
| **Positive** | 2,510 | 1,572 | 2,783 | 22,233 |
| **Neutral** | 3,363 | 1,640 | 2,312 | 22,721 |
| **Negative** | 1,023 | 601 | 2,124 | 15,844 |
| **Total** | 6,896 | 3,813 | 7,219 | 60,798 |

Table 3: Datasets distribution in number of tweets.

We chose these datasets because they are publicly available to the research community, they have been used several times in sentiment analysis competitions, and they are very different from each other, in terms of size, language, topic, and annotation process. For each dataset separately, a lexicon and a supervised model is generated using the train examples, and the model created is evaluated using the test examples.

The results of our experiments are shown in Table 4. We do not use *accuracy* because it is not a good measure for text categorisation when using an imbalanced corpus Yang1999. Instead, we use the F1 (F-score with $\beta=1$) because it represents a balance between precision and recall of the measures of each polarity. Moreover, the F1

[10] http://alt.qcri.org/semeval2015/

[11] http://www.daedalus.es/TASS2014/

scores shown are the macro-average of all the F1 scores of the polarities, as it gives the same importance to all polarities regardless of the number of examples in the dataset. The *Parameters* column refers to the *n* and *k* values employed for the k-skip-n-grams generation. However, for simplicity, the parameter *n* will represent the *maximum* number of terms allowed in a skipgram. For example, the experiments with $n$=3 will include skipgrams with $n$=3, $n$=2 and $n$=1. The notation $n$=*max* indicates there was no limit with the number of terms, and $k$=*max* indicates there was no restriction with the number of skips.

| Parameters | TASS | SemEval |
|---|---|---|
| $n$=2 | 0.636 | 0.543 |
| $n$=2,$k$=1 | 0.642 | 0.548 |
| $n$=2,$k$=2 | 0.646 | 0.551 |
| $n$=2,$k$=3 | **0.647** | **0.560** |
| $n$=2,$k$=*max* | **0.647** | 0.553 |
| $n$=3 | 0.624 | 0.491 |
| $n$=3,$k$=1 | 0.623 | 0.489 |
| $n$=3,$k$=2 | 0.630 | 0.493 |
| $n$=3,$k$=3 | 0.637 | **0.512** |
| $n$=3,$k$=*max* | **0.639** | 0.491 |

Table 4: Results of the evaluation (F1 score)

The evaluation performed with the TASS dataset shows a benefit in the use of skipgrams. The best F1 score was obtained with $n$=2 and $k$=3 (or $k$=*max*) respect the results obtained with bigrams, with an improvement of 1.7%, and with $n$=3 and $k$=*max* respect the results obtained with trigrams, with an improvement of 2.4%. In the case of the evaluation performed with the SemEval dataset, the benefit is bigger. The best F1 score was obtained with $n$=2 and $k$=3 (or $k$=*max*) respect the results obtained with bigrams, with an improvement of 3.1%, and with $n$=3 and $k$=3 respect the results obtained with trigrams, with an improvement of 4.2%. It can thus be suggested that there are some sentiment-specific expressions that do not appear together in some cases and the skipgram modelling has discovered, useful to determine the polarity of a text. Even tough the size, topic, language, and annotation process of these datasets is very different, the evaluation shows a robust improvement with the usage of skipgrams in both datasets.

## 5 Conclusions

In this paper we presented a supervised hybrid approach for Sentiment Analysis in Twitter. We built a sentiment lexicon from a polarity dataset using statistical measures. We employed skipgrams as information units, to enrich the sentiment lexicon with combinations of words that do not appear explicitly in the text. The lexicon created was used in conjunction with machine learning techniques to create a polarity classifier.

The evaluation was carried out against very different datasets, in terms of size, topic, language, and annotation process, and showed an improvement with the usage of skipgrams in all datasets. More specifically, just increasing the maximum allowed number of gaps between the words in the skipgrams ($k$), the results obtained were up to a 3.1% better. This suggested that there are some sentiment-specific combinations of words discovered by the skipgram modelling, that do not appear explicitly together.

As future work, we plan to study new methods to calculate and combine the weight of the skipgrams. In addition, we want to include external resources and tools, such as a more complex normalisation, or knowledge from existing sentiment lexicons like SentiWordNet. We will also extend our study to different corpora and domains, to confirm the robustness of the approach.

## Acknowledgments

This research work has been partially funded by the Spanish Government and the European Commission through the project, ATTOS (TIN2012-38536-C03- 03), LEGOLANG (TIN2012-31224), SAM (FP7- 611312) and FIRST (FP7-287607).

## References

Nora Aranberri, Pablo Gamallo, and Lluis Padr. 2013.Introduccio´ n a la tarea compartida Tweet-Norm 2013: normalización léxica de tuits en español. In XXIX Congreso de la Sociedad Española de Procesamiento de Lenguaje Natural (SEPLN 2013).

Chih-chung Chang and Chih-jen Lin. 2011. LIBSVM: A Library for Support Vector Machines. ACM Transactions on Intelligent Systems and Technology (TIST), 2:1–39.

Ferm´ın L Cruz, Jose A Troyano, Fernando Enríquez, F Javier Ortega, and Carlos G Vallejo. 2013. Long autonomy or long delay? the importance of domain in opinion mining. Expert Systems with Applications, 40(8):3174–3184.

Javi Fernández, Yoan Gutiérrez, José M. Gómez, and Patricio Martínez-Barco. 2014. GPLSI: Supervised Sentiment Analysis in Twitter using Skipgrams. In Proceedings of the 8th International Workshop on Semantic Evaluation (SemEval 2014), number Se- mEval, pages 294–299.

David Guthrie, Ben Allison, Wei Liu, Louise Guthrie, and Yorick Wilks. 2006. A Closer Look at Skip- gram Modelling. In 5th international Conference on Language Resources and Evaluation (LREC 2006), pages 1–4.

Soo-min Kim, Marina Rey, and Eduard Hovy. 2004. Determining the Sentiment of Opinions. In Pro- ceedings of the 20th International Conference on Computational Linguistics (COLING 2004), page 1367.

Walaa Medhat, Ahmed Hassan, and Hoda Korashy. 2014. Sentiment Analysis Algorithms and Appli- cations: a Survey. Ain Shams Engineering Journal.

Saif M. Mohammad, Svetlana Kiritchenko, and Xiao- dan Zhu. 2013. NRC-Canada: Building the State- of-the-Art in Sentiment Analysis of Tweets. In Pro- ceedings of the International Workshop on Semantic Evaluation (SemEval-2013).

Preslav Nakov, Sara Rosenthal, Alan Ritter, and Theresa Wilson. 2013. SemEval-2013 Task 2: Sentiment Analysis in Twitter. In Proceedings of the International Workshop on Semantic Evaluation (SemEval-2013), volume 2, pages 312–320.

Bo Pang and Lillian Lee. 2008. Opinion Mining and Sentiment Analysis. Foundations and Trends in Information Retrieval, 2(1–2):1–135.

Sara Rosenthal and Alan Ritter. 2014. SemEval-2014 Task 9 : Sentiment Analysis in Twitter. In Proceed- ings of the 8th International Workshop on Semantic Evaluation (SemEval 2014), pages 73–80.

Hassan Saif, Yulan He, and Harith Alani. 2012. Sen- timent Analysis of Twitter. In Proceedings of the 11th International Semantic Web Conference (ISWC 2012), pages 11–15.

Fabrizio Sebastiani. 2002. Machine Learning in Au- tomated Text Categorization. ACM Computing Sur- veys (CSUR), 34(1):1–47, March.

Maite Taboada, Julian Brooke, Milan Tofiloski, Kim- berly Voll, and Manfred Stede. 2011. Lexicon- based methods for sentiment analysis. Computa- tional Linguistics, 37(2):267–307.

Songbo Tan, Xueqi Cheng, Yuefen Wang, and Hongbo Xu. 2009. Adapting Naive Bayes to Domain Adap- tation for Sentiment Analysis. Advances in Informa- tion Retrieval, pages 337–349.

Julio Villena-Roma´n and Janine Garcıa-Morera. 2013. TASS 2013-Workshop on Sentiment Analysis at SE- PLN 2013: An overview. In XXIX Congreso de la Sociedad Española de Procesamiento de Lenguaje Natural (SEPLN 2013).

Julio Villena-Roman, Eugenio Martınez-Camara, Sara Lana-Serrano, and Jose Carlos Gonzalez-Cristobal. 2013. TASS - Workshop on Sentiment Analysis at SEPLN. Procesamiento del Lenguaje Natural, 50:37–44.

Yiming Yang and Xin Liu. 1999. A re-examination of text categorization methods. Proceedings of the 22nd annual international ACM SIGIR conference on Research and development in information re- trieval (SIGIR 1999), pages 42–49.

# Emotion Detection from text: A Survey

Lea Canales, Patricio Martínez-Barco
Department of Software and Computing Systems
University of Alicante
{lcanales,patricio}@dlsi.ua.es

Abstract

This survey describes recent works in the field of Emotion Detection from text, being a part of the broader area of *Affective Computing*. This survey has been inspired on the well-known fact that, despite there is a lot of work on emotional detection systems, a lot of work is expected to be done yet. The increment of these systems is due to the large amount of emotional data available in Social Web. Detecting emotions from text have attracted the attention of many researchers in computational linguistics because it has a wide range of applications, such as suicide prevention or measuring well-being of a community. This paper mainly collects works based on lexical and machine learning approaches and these works are classificated in accordance with the emotional model and the approach used.

## 1 Introduction

This survey describes recent works in the field of emotion or affect detection from text. Emotion detection is part of the broader area of *Affective Computing* with aims to enable computers recognize and express emotions (Picard 1997). Current affect detection systems are with respect to individual modalities or channels, such as face, voice and text (Calvo 2010). In this survey, we have focused on reviewing works about emotion detection from text.

Emotion detection and analysis has been widely researched in neuroscience, psychology and behavior science, as they are an important element of human nature. In computer science, this task has also attracted the attention of many researchers, especially in the field of human computer interactions (Strapparava 2008).

In computational linguistics, the detection of emotion states of a person by analyzing a text document written by him/her can have many applications in different fields, such as in e-learning environment (Rodriguez 2012) or suicide prevention (Desmet 2013, Vaassen 2014). For this reason, we decided to develop a survey about emotion detection systems from text and make it available to researcher community.

In this survey, we classify the most relevant emotion detection works in accordance with the emotional model and the approach used. A numerical comparison is not possible since each work used different data sets to evaluate their systems.

Regarding the search strategy used in the survey, we have looked for all of papers related to emotion detection from text in different research databases like *Scopus*[12] or *IEEE Xplore*[13]. Later on, we have reviewed the papers obtained of these databases and have selected the best papers that use lexical approach or machine learning approach in their emotion detection systems. The selection criterion used is based on the relevance of each work in the field of *Affective Computing*.

This paper is organized as follows. In section 2, describes the emotional models. Section 3, the different computational approaches for emotion detection is described. Finally, in section 4, we express our conclusions about this survey.

## 2 Emotion models

When emotional detection systems are analyzed, it is important to focus our interest on describing and explaining how the emotion models are established, as they are, the basis of these systems.

According to research in psychology, there is a number of theories about how to represent emotions (Cowie 2003) but two are the most important and the most often used in existing approaches in Sentiment Analysis (Francisco 2013): *emotional categories* and *emotional dimensions*.

[12] http://www.scopus.com/

[13] http://ieeexplore.ieee.org/

*Emotional categories* approaches are focused on model emotions based on distinct emotion classes or labels. The categorical model assumes that there are discrete emotion categories. The Ekman's basic emotion model is within this approach. (Ekman 1999) concluded that the six basic emotions are ANGER, DISGUST, FEAR, HAPPINESS, SADNESS and SURPRISE. (Plutchik 1980) define a set of eight basic bipolar emotions, consisting of a superset of Ekman's and with two additions: TRUST and ANTICIPATION. These eight emotions are organized into four bipolar sets: joy vs. sadness, anger vs. fear, trust vs. disgust, and surprise vs. anticipation.

*Emotional dimensions* approaches represent affects in a dimensional form. Each emotion occupies a location in this space (Kim 2011). One of the more representative model of these approaches is (Russell 1980). Rusell's Circumplex Model of Affect suggests that emotions are distributed in a two-dimensional circular space: valence dimension and arousal dimension, as show Figure 1. The valence dimension indicates how much PLEASANT and UNPLEASANT is an emotion. The arousal dimension differentiates ACTIVATION and DEACTIVATION states. In this approach, we also find the Mehrabian's model, a model based on a three-dimensional PAD (Pleasure – Arousal - Dominance) representation (Mehrabian 1996). The dominance dimension indicates whether the subject feels in control of the situation or not.

Although existing emotional categories and emotional dimensions for representing affective states, categorical approaches are the most commonly used (Calvo 2013), as we can check out in next section. Most of computational approaches are based on emotional categories, due to its simplicity and familiarity. Nevertheless, emotional categories may not cover all emotions adequately because emotion categories are limited. This is a major benefit of emotional dimensional models. They are not correlated to a certain emotional state and are able to capture subtle emotion concepts that differ only slightly. In addition, a dimensional emotion model provides a means for measuring similarity between affective states (Kim 2011).

As we can observe, there are not an emotion model better than other. Both models have advantages and disadvantages. The election of an emotion model depends on the set of emotions that we want detect.

## 3 Computational approaches for emotion detection

Emotion detection techniques can be divided into lexicon based approaches and machine learning approaches. On the one hand, lexicon based approaches rely on lexical resources such as lexicons, bags of words or ontologies. On the other hand, Machine Learning (ML) approaches apply ML algorithms based on linguistic features.

Figure 1: Graphical representation of the Circumplex Model of Affect.

### 3.1 Lexicon-based approaches

Lexicon based approaches are approaches that only use one or several lexical resources to detect emotions detection.

Among these approaches, we can find *keyword-based approaches* that are based on predetermining a set of terms to classify the text into emotion categories. In (Strapparava 2008), as a baseline, they implemented a simple algorithm that checked the presence of affective words in the headlines, and computed a score that reflected the frequency of the words in this affective lexicon in the text. They used WordNet-Affect (Strapparava 2004).

Also among Lexicon based approaches, we find the *ontology-based ones*. (Balahur 2011) use EmotiNet - a resource for the detection of emotion from text based on commonsense knowledge on concepts, their interaction and their affective consequence – to detect emotion. EmotiNet models situations as chains of actions and their corresponding emotional effect using an ontological representation. Their evaluation consists in testing if by employing the model they build and the knowledge contained in the core of EmotiNet, they are able to detect the emotion expressed in new examples pertaining to the categories in International Survey of Emotional Antecedents and Reactions (ISEAR), through computing the similarity between the emotion chain of the new situation and the EmotiNet emotion chains. Their evaluation shows that the structure and content of EmotiNet are appropriate to address the automatic treatment of implicitly expressed affect. (Sykora 2013) also use an ontology approach to solve the problem of fine-grained emotion detection in text. Their approach detects a range of eight high-level emotions; anger, confusion, disgust, fear, happiness, sadness, shame and surprise.

*Statistical approach* is also considered as a Lexical approach. Most knowledge-based works use Latent Semantic Analysis (LSA), a statistical approach for analyzing the relationships between a set of documents and the terms mentioned in these documents in order to produce a set of meaningful patterns related to the documents and terms (Deerwester 1999). (Gill 2008) used LSA and the Hyperspace Analogue to Language (HAL) to automatically compute the semantic similarity between the texts and emotions keywords. Recently, (Wang 2013) propose a method that uses an improved LSA algorithm for text emotion classification on ISEAR dataset.

## 3.2 Machine Learning-based approaches

Machine learning is a scientific discipline that deals with the construction and study of algorithms that can learn from data (Kovahi 1998). Such algorithms operate by building a model based on inputs and using these inputs to make predictions or decisions, rather than following only explicitly programmed instructions (Bishop 2006).

Specifically in emotion detection, Machine learning algorithms are used to learn how detect emotions. These approaches can be divided into *supervised* and *unsupervised learning*.

*Supervised learning* approaches rely on a labelled training data, a set of training examples. The supervised learning algorithm analyses the training data and infers a function, which we use for mapping new examples (Mohri 2012).

A labelled corpus is a large and structured set of text that it is necessary annotated with emotional tags. In this case, the annotation process is considered as one of their most important disadvantages as it becomes a tedious and time-consuming task. However, there are recent works related with emotion detection in Twitter messages, where the training examples are automatically labelled through hashtags and emoticons contained. (Hasan 2014, Wang 2012, Roberts 2012, Suttles 2013) among others, are proposals that use this method for labeling training data automatically. Moreover, (Hasan 2014a) confirms that hashtags are indeed good emotion labels.

Concerning works that apply supervised learning algorithms, we can find both the categorical and the dimensional approaches to base their emotional models. Categorical approaches are the most commonly used in emotion detection (Calvo 2013). One of the first works based in this model is (Alm 2005). This proposal presented an empirical study of applying supervised machine learning with the SNoW learning architecture (Roth 1999). They used an annotated corpus with an extended set of Ekman basic emotions. (Strapparava 2008), in one of the experiment presented in their work, applied Naïve Bayes classifier trained on the blog entries from LiveJournal.com [14]. They used a collection of blogposts annotated with Ekman's emotions. More recently, (Balabantaray 2012) presents an Emotion classifier that is able to determinate the emotion class of the person writing. Their emotion classifier is based on multi-class SVM kernels and takes decisions according to the basic emotions identified by Ekman (Ekman 1999). (Roberts 2012) also use the Ekman's six basic emotions and include `LOVE` emotion. Their system uses a series of binary SVM classifiers to detect

[14] http://www.livejournal.com/

each of the seven emotions. Other related work with categorical emotion models, (Suttles 2013) classify emotions according to a set of eight basic bipolar emotions defined by Plutchick. This allows them to treat the multi-class problem of emotion classification as a binary problem for opposing emotion pairs. Their approach applies *Distant Supervision* (Mintz 2009).

About works that apply supervised learning approach and use dimensional emotion model, we can find the work of (Hasan 2014), where they propose an approach for automatically classifying text messages of individual to infer their emotional states. They use the Rusell's Circumplex Model of Affect as emotion model and train supervised classifiers to detect multiple emotion. Specifically, they have compared the accuracy of SVM, KNN, Decision Tree and Naïve Bayes for classifying Twitter messages.

Regarding *unsupervised learning* approaches, these algorithms try to find hidden structure in unlabeled data in order to build models for emotion classification (Mohri 2012).

As occurs in supervised learning, among unsupervised learning proposals also it can be found systems based on categorical and dimensional emotion models.

With respect to works based in categorical emotion model, (Strapparava 2008) apply unsupervised techniques combining LSA with WordNet Affect (Strapparava 2004). This proposal used the Ekman's basic emotions. (Agrawal 2012) proposes a novel unsupervised context-based approach based on a methodology that does not depend on any existing affect lexicon, thereby their model is flexible enough to classify sentences beyond Ekman's model of six basic emotions. (Calvo 2013) presents different categorical approaches based on Vector Space Model (VSM) with three dimensionality reduction techniques: Latent Semantic Analysis (LSA), Probabilistic Latent Semantic Analysis (PLSA) and Non-negative Matrix Factorization (NMF). This work conclude that NMF-based categorical classification performs the best among categorical approaches to classification.

About unsupervised approach with dimensional emotion model, we find (Calvo 2013). This work used a normative database ANEW (Bradley 1999) to produce tree-dimensional vectors (valence, arousal, dominance) for each pseudo-document.

The articles presented in this survey are summarized in Table 1.

## 4 Conclusion

In this survey, we have started discussing the emotion models defined by psychologies because it is the base of emotion detection. As concluding by (Calvo 2013) and we have check out, categorical approach is the model more used in emotion detection systems.

Regarding Lexical approaches, *keyword-based approaches* are easily implementable and we can obtain good accuracy values, even though this approach has drawbacks: determining the content of the emotion lexicon is subjective, obtaining wrong recall values and the select words may be ambiguous (Suttles 2013). Moreover, it is not suitable for wide range of domains.

With respect to *approaches based on ontologies* let us use commonsense knowledge and improve recall values but the creation of an emotional ontology is a tedious and time-consuming task.

Consequently, lexical resources usually are used as features in Machine Learning algorithms.

As for *Machine Learning approaches*, the supervised learning approach is more used in emotion detection because it usually leads to better results than unsupervised learning (Kim 2011). Although, these approaches need labelling training examples and annotating of examples, which is a time-consuming task. For this reason, several researches have analyzed as

| Papers | Categories | Emotion Model | Approaches |
|---|---|---|---|
| (Strapparava and Mihalcea, 2008) | Anger, Disgust, Fear, Joy, Sadness, Surprise | Categorical | Lexical-based |
| (Gill et al., 2008) | Anger, Fear, Surprise, Joy, Anticipation, Acceptance, Sadness, Disgust | Categorical | Lexical-based |
| (Balahur et al., 2011) | Anger, Disgust, Fear, Guilt, Joy, Sadness, Shame | Categorical | Lexical-based |
| (Sykora et al., 2013) | Anger, Confusion, Disgust, Fear, Happiness, Sadness, Shame, Surprise | Categorical | Lexical-based |
| (Wang and Zheng, 2013) | Anger, Disgust, Fear, Guilt, Joy, Sadness, Shame | Categorical | Lexical-based |
| (Alm et al., 2005) | Anger, Disgust, Fear, Happiness, Sadness, Positively Surprise, Negatively Suprise | Categorical | Supervised Learning-based |
| (Strapparava and Mihalcea, 2008) | Anger, Disgust, Fear, Joy, Sadness, Surprise | Categorical | Supervised Learning-based |
| (Balabantaray et al., 2012) | Anger, Disgust, Fear, Happiness, Sadness, Surprise | Categorical | Supervised Learning-based |
| (Roberts et al., 2012) | Anger, Disgust, Fear, Joy, Sadness, Surprise, Love | Categorical | Supervised Learning-based |
| (Suttles and Ide, 2013) | Anger, Disgust, Fear, Happiness, Sadness, Surprise, Trust, Anticipation | Categorical | Supervised Learning-based |
| (Hasan et al., 2014b) | Happy-Active, Happy-Inactive, Unhappy-Active, Unhappy-Inactive | Dimensional | Supervised Learning-based |
| (Strapparava and Mihalcea, 2008) | Anger, Disgust, Fear, Joy, Sadness, Surprise | Categorical | Unsupervised Learning-based |
| (Agrawal and An, 2012) | Anger, Disgust, Fear, Happiness, Sadness, Surprise | Categorical | Unsupervised Learning-based |
| (Calvo and Kim, 2013) | Anger-Disgust, Fear, Joy, Sadness | Categorical | Unsupervised Learning-based |
| (Calvo and Kim, 2013) | Anger-Disgust, Fear, Joy, Sadness | Dimensional | Unsupervised Learning-based |

Table 1: Emotion Detection approaches

realize this task automatically and when our system process Twitter messages, the messages can be annotated through hashtags or emotions that it contains.

Although unsupervised learning approach leads worse results than supervised learning, it can be a good election for the emotion detection task because the emotional interpretations of a text can be highly subjective and the annotation task is an error prone task (Kim 2011).

In conclusion, Machine Learning approaches are better option for detection emotion task since we obtain a model is also able to detect emotions in texts that have only an indirect reference to an emotions. Although, it is important use a good lexical resource as features in Machine Learning algorithms to obtain good results.

Concerning pending tasks in emotion detection field, we consider really important that researcher community establish an annotated corpus and a set of metrics that it may be used to evaluate the different existing systems and the future systems. Moreover, in emotional detection systems based on machine learning approach, we have detected that most of these systems use features based on a shallow analysis on the text as: n-grams, punctuation, emoticons or

Part-Of-Speech. Hence, we propose a new direction focuses on deep analysis, since we consider that if we use features based on a deep analyis on the text we could improve the emotional detection systems.

based on a deep analysis on the text we could improve the emotional detection systems.

## Acknowledgments

This research has been supported by the FPI grant (BES-2013-065950) from the Spanish Ministry of Science and Innovation, under the project LEGOLANGUAGE (TIN2012-31224) funded by the Spanish Government. It has been also funded by the Valencian Government (grant no. PROMETEOII/2014/001).

## References

Ameeta Agrawal and Aijun An. 2012. Unsupervised Emotion Detection from Text Using Semantic and Syntactic Relations. In 2012 IEEE/WIC/ACM International Conferences on Web Intelligence and Intelligent Agent Technology, pages 346–353. IEEE Computer Society, December.

Cecilia Ovesdotter Alm, Dan Roth, and Richard Sproat. 2005. Emotions from text: machine learning for text-based emotion prediction. Proc. Conf. Human Language Technology and Empirical Methods in Natural Language Processing, pages 579–586.

R C Balabantaray, Mudasir Mohammad, and Nibha Sharma. 2012. Multi-Class Twitter Emotion Classification: A New Approach. International Journal of Applied Information Systems (IJAIS), 4(1):48–53.

Alexandra Balahur, Jesús M. Hermida, and Andrés Montoyo. 2011. Detecting Implicit Expressions of Sentiment in Text Based on Commonsense Knowledge. In 2nd Workshop on Computational Approaches to Subjectivity and Sentiment Analysis, ACL-HLT 2011, pages 53–60.

C. M. Bishop. 2006. Pattern Recognition and Machine Learning. Springer. Margaret M Bradley and Peter J Lang. 1999. Affective Norms for English Words (ANEW): Instruction Manual and Affective Ratings. Technical report, The Center for Research in Psychophysiology, University of Florida.

Rafael A Calvo and Sunghwan Mac Kim. 2013. Emotions in text: dimensional and categorical models. Computational Intelligence, 29(3).

Rafael A Calvo and Senior Member. 2010. Affect Detection: An Interdisciplinary Review of Models, Methods, and Their Applications. IEEE Transactions on Affective Computing, 1(1):18–37.

Roddy Cowie and Randolph R. Cornelius. 2003. Describing the emotional states that are expressed in speech. Speech Communication, 40(1-2):5–32, April.

Scott Deerwester, Susan T. Dumais, George W. Furnas, Thomas K. Landauer, and Richard Harshman.1999. Indexing by latent semantic analysis. Journal of the American Society for Information Science, 41(6):391–407, September.

Bart Desmet and Véronique Hoste. 2013. Emotion detection in suicide notes. Expert Systems with Applications, 40(16):6351–6358, November.

Paul Ekman. 1999. Basic emotions. In Handbook of cognition and emotion, pages 45–60. Virginia Francisco and Pablo Gerv´as. 2013. EmoTag: An Approach to Automated Mark-Up of Emotions in Texts. Computational Intelligence, 29(4):680–721.

Alastair J. Gill, Robert M. French, Darren Gergle, and Jon Oberlander. 2008. Identifying Emotional Characteristics from Short Blog Texts. In 30th Annual Meeting of the Cognitive Science Society, pages 2237–2242.

Maryam Hasan, Emmanuel Agu, and Elke Rundensteiner. 2014a. Using Hashtags as Labels for Supervised Learning of Emotions in Twitter Messages.

Maryam Hasan, Elke Rundensteiner, and Emmanuel Agu. 2014b. EMOTEX: Detecting Emotions in Twitter Messages. In ASE BIGDATA/SOCIALCOM/CYBERSECURI TY Conference, pages 27–31.

Sunghwan Mac Kim. 2011. Recognising Emotions and Sentiments in Text. Ph.D. thesis, University of Sydney.

Ron Kovahi and Foster Provost. 1998. Glossary of terms. Machine Learning, pages 271–274.

A. Mehrabian. 1996. Pleasure-arousal-dominance: A general framework for describing and measuring individual.

Current Psychology, 15(4):505–525. M. Mintz, S. Bills, R. Snow, and D. Jurafsky. 2009. Distant supervision for relation extraction without labeled data. In Proceedings of the Joint Conference of the 47th Annual Meeting of the ACL and the 4th International Joint Conference on Natural Language Processing of the AFNLP, pages 1003–1011.

Mehryar Mohri, Afshin Rostamizadeh, and Ameet Talwalkar. 2012. Foundations of Machine Learning. MIT Press.

Rosalind W. Picard. 1997. Affective computing. MIT Press Cambridge, MA, USAc 1997. R. Plutchik. 1980. Emotion: Theory, Research and Experience. In Theories of emotion, volume 11, page 399. Academic Press.

Kirk Roberts, Michael A Roach, Joseph Johnson, Josh Guthrie, and Sanda M Harabagiu. 2012. EmpaTweet: Annotating and Detecting Emotions on Twitter. In Nicoletta Calzolari (Conference Chair) Piperidis, Khalid Choukri, Thierry Declerck, Mehmet U˘gur Do˘gan, Bente Maegaard, Joseph Mariani, Asuncion Moreno, Jan Odijk, and Stelios, editors, Proceedings of the Eight International Conference on Language Resources and Evaluation (LREC'12). European Language Resources Association (ELRA).

Pilar Rodriguez, Alvaro Ortigosa, and Rosa M. Carro. 2012. Extracting Emotions from Texts in ELearning Environments. In 2012 Sixth International Conference on Complex, Intelligent, and Software Intensive Systems, pages 887–892. Ieee, July.

Dan Roth, Chad Cumby, Andy Carlson, and Jeff Rosen. 1999. The SNoW Learning Architecture. Technical report, UIUC Computer Science Department. J.A. Russell. 1980. A circumplex model of affect. Journal of Personality and Social Psychology, 39(6):1161–1178.

Carlo Strapparava and Rada Mihalcea. 2008. Learning to identify emotions in text. In Proceedings of the 2008 ACM symposium on Applied computing - SAC '08, pages 1556–1560, New York, New York, USA. ACM Press.

Carlo Strapparava and Alessandro Valitutti. 2004. WordNet-Affect: an Affective Extension of Word-Net. In 4th International Conference on Language Resources and Evaluation, pages 1083–1086.

Jared Suttles and Nancy Ide. 2013. Distant Supervision for Emotion Classification with Discrete Binary Values. In Alexander Gelbukh, editor, Computational Linguistics and Intelligent Text Processing, volume 7817 of Lecture Notes in Computer Science, pages 121–136. Springer Berlin Heidelberg, Berlin, Heidelberg.

Martin D Sykora, Thomas W Jackson, and Suzanne Elayan. 2013. Emotive ontology: extracting finegrained emotions from terse, informal messages. IADIS International Journal on Computer Science and Information Systems, 8(2):106–118. Frederik Vaassen. 2014. Measuring emotion. Ph.D. thesis, Universiteit Antwerpen.

Xuren Wang and Qiuhui Zheng. 2013. Text Emotion Classification Research Based on Improved Latent Semantic Analysis Algorithm. In Proceedings of the 2nd International Conference on Computer Science nd Electronics Engineering (ICCSEE 2013), number Iccsee, pages 210–213, Paris, France. Atlantis Press.

Wenbo Wang, Lu Chen, Krishnaprasad Thirunarayan, and Amit P. Sheth. 2012. Harnessing Twitter "Big Data" for Automatic Emotion Identification. In 2012 International Conference on Privacy, Security,Risk and Trust and 2012 International Conference on Social Computing, pages 587–592. IEEE Computer Society, September.

**Association for Computational Linguistics**
209 N. Eighth Street
Stroudsburg, Pennsylvania 18360

proceedings.com

# 13th Conference of the European Chapter of the Association for Computational Linguistics 2012 (EACL 2012)

## Student Research Workshop

Avignon, France
23 – 27 April 2012

ISBN: 978-1-62276-501-0